.com
thelordismyshepherd

Seeking God in Cyberspace

Joshua Hammerman

An Imprint of Health Communications, Inc.®

Deerfield Beach, Florida
www.simchapress.com
www.thelordismyshepherd.com

Library of Congress Catalog Card Number: 00-057251

©2000 Joshua Hammerman
ISBN 1-55874-821-0

Publisher: Simcha Press
             An Imprint of Health Communications, Inc.
             3201 S.W. 15th Street
             Deerfield Beach, FL 33442-8190

Cover design by Lisa Camp
Inside book design by Dawn Grove

Contents

Acknowledgments

This book could not have been written without the inspiration of so many teachers, including those at places where I've studied (Brown University, the Jewish Theological Seminary and NYU) and those whose wisdom I've encountered elsewhere along my life's path. They are too numerous to mention (let's just say that I could begin with Moses and Confucius and move on from there), but each bit of understanding that I've accumulated over my forty-three years can trace its roots to the influence of a teacher who has been special to my life. Those of my mentors who are alive and manage to find this book will certainly recognize the imprint of their ideas on my own thoughts.

I'm also indebted to my congregants and professional colleagues for their constant support and for sharing their lives with me, for the past thirteen years in Stamford, and previously in Peekskill and Beacon, New York. I've always felt that my rabbinical work and my writing have been mutually enriching. My congregants and friends have never let me stray too far from the hard, human issues of the real world, but they have also allowed me the space to nurture my inner life. Within my community, several people have also given needed advice and assistance in the preparation of this book, including Dr. Alvin Rosenfeld, Tracy Daniels and Mitchell Levitz, who shared their considerable expertise, Charles (Chick) Finder, my photographer, and Andrew D. Lehrfeld of Out-of-Site, Inc., who has developed the book's Website at *www.thelordismyshepherd.com.*

I am especially grateful to those who have shown great faith in my work over the years and, through that confidence, have made this publication possible. Among this group I must include Rabbi Michael Schorin, Gary Rosenblatt of the *Jewish Week,* Eric Copage of the *New York Times,* and most especially my agent, Mel Berger of the William Morris Agency. I am also very grateful to Deborah Broide and Carolyn Hessel for their help in promoting this book. The assistance of Sandee Brawarsky of the *Jewish Week* was also indispensable in bringing this book to light.

The people from Simcha Press/HCI are an author's dream. They are helpful, enthusiastic and encouraging. My thanks to all of them, in particular Kim Weiss, Lisa Drucker and Erica Orloff, Matthew Diener, Susan Tobias, Larry Getlen, Judy Perry and the sales and marketing staff.

And then there is my family. In this book I speak of how the Internet has brought my family closer together. This is true, but the centrality of family is something that I learned long ago from my parents, Michal (of blessed memory) and Miriam Hammerman, and a lesson later reinforced by my in-laws, Howard (of blessed memory) and Gloria Aisenberg. I thank them, and my siblings and extended family as well.

An inspiration to me throughout the writing of this book was my cousin Jeffrey Avick, who died of AIDS just a few months ago. In many ways, this book is a tribute to his brilliance as a writer, his zest for life and his ability to see the Internet as a way to enhance relationship.

Imagine having a rabbi, who works impossibly long hours, as your father or husband. Then imagine knowing that your husband/father spends much of his precious "leisure" time sating his passion for writing. That is the predicament my wife, Mara, and sons Ethan and Daniel have faced, and yet each morning they greet me with that special smile and at the end of the day with lots of hugs. And they seem to know that, in spite of it all, they are the defining, immutable fact of my life. For me, everything else revolves around my beloved wife and children.

I dedicate this book in memory of my father, Cantor Michal Hammerman, who died tragically at age sixty, but whose memory lives on in cyberspace and, now, in print. On his memorial stone is an inscription from Psalms that has been the guiding credo of my life, and consequently of this book:

> *Shiru l'Adonai shir hadash.*
> *Sing unto the Lord a new song.*

Once you've read this book, join us at our Website, *www.thelordismyshepherd.com*. I'll be posting updated information on the sites visited in this book, as well as new ones I've visited during subsequent online quests. From this site you can contact me directly to share your questions and passions. And there you can share with other readers the details of your own cyberjourneys.

Introduction
God Unfolding: Preparing for the Journey

You are about to experience the Internet in a way that is both very new and very old, as a modern-day sacred text, a source of spiritual inspiration and fulfillment. As the world of cyberspace has increasingly become part of our daily lives, it has become, for many, a public library and shopping mall, a post office and entertainment center. In this book, the Internet is seen as a catalyst for worship and introspection. This is not to say that one should bow down to the computer on your desk as some metallic Baal or Zeus. This is merely to suggest that the Internet can help us experience and approach God.

I take two very different approaches to this task in these pages: one is experiential and the other more analytic and expository. In those chapters where this subject is discussed analytically, I first consider the general question of whether spirituality and technology are compatible, then present a wide variety of ways to perceive sanctity within this new technology we call the Internet. Some of the arguments are straightforward, others more complex; some involve mainstream religious ways of understanding God, others take a more mystical perspective. As we delve deeper and deeper, getting closer and closer to the core of the subject, we are led to the startling conclusion that the true essence of God can be understood—indeed most plausibly is seen—as being *digital in nature*.

The experiential approach is both the most risky and unique,[1] and it is reflected in the even-numbered chapters appearing in sans serif type. These consist of a series of three actual online spiritual journeys I have taken. Through these journeys, which are chronicled primarily in a stream-of-consciousness format, I attempt to model a new form of spiritual exploration; call it "the virtual pilgrimage," if you will. The reflections recorded here provide a running journal of my spiritual struggles and fears, and moments of epiphany and amazement while journeying online. I've tried as much as possible to present these chapters as raw religious data, hoping that, while all the details of my journey may not parallel yours, there will be moments of deep resonance for you. At the very least, I will have shared a valuable tool that might be helpful to your own growth. Having completed three journeys for this book and others on my own, I believe we are on to a new means of utilizing the vast power of this new technology to connect us to all of Reality.

The medieval Jewish mystics known as kabbalists believed that existence is multilayered. That is, God's presence becomes more manifest through the unfolding of Creation. Similarly, our ability to perceive God increases as we penetrate deeper into anything we encounter, be it a force of nature, a personal relationship, a text or, for that matter, a Website. So while we are diving into the Web to find God, let us imagine ourselves coming across some buried treasure covered by a multilayered casement of barnacles and seaweed. As we dive from site to site, we are in fact peeling away at those outer layers, and within each site itself, we also peel away at the superficial in order to find what is most essential, which is often what is most hidden.

If we are to treat the Internet as a sacred tableau and what appears on our screen as a sacred text, then it should be possible to employ time-tested exegetical techniques to allow God's essence to unfold. We'll be doing that here.

So join me now as we travel through a world that transcends time and space, built upon the elements of Creation. Using the tools of ancient wisdom, modern technology and plain, old gut instinct, we are ready to begin an adventure that our grandparents could not have imagined, a pilgrimage without dust. Who knows where we will end up?

I encourage you to read the experiential chapters while online, if Internet access is available to you. I cannot guarantee that all the sites I present will be accessible to you. In fact, given that the only constant in cyberspace is change, I guarantee that a number of the sites will not be available. Even in the few months between the time I originally took these journeys and the completion of this book, much change has occurred. Were I to follow the same path today, the results would be quite different. But that's what makes it so exciting and unpredictable. Still, you'll be able to follow along better if, at least occasionally, we are both looking at the same thing. And what's most important is that if you are reading these chapters while online, you can always put the book down from time to time and go off on your own. This is meant to be both an interactive reading experience and a catalyst for your own spiritual explorations.

Serendipity is the key to finding God on the Web. When you least expect it, God will be there. I hope you'll also sense the haphazard, what-lies-hidden-around-the-corner sensation that I had as I moved from site to site. I suspect that you'll discover, as I did, that like the evolving process of Creation, the true meaning of one site might not be understood until you've reached the next, or the last, or not at all. I suspect that you'll be amazed, as I was, at seeing how the digital universe unfolds in a manner similar to the cosmos envisioned by the ancient mystics, one that aims remarkably toward equilibrium and harmony, a balance of the male and female, between justice and mercy, good and evil. You'll sense the organic nature of reality, how seemingly unrelated things are in fact intimately connected. You'll see signs of the supreme value of life and the defeat of death, the establishment of order and the conquest of chaos. Together, we'll look for God and look to discern God's will. We'll look, in the end, for clues to our own mission and destiny.

Since we won't need to walk, we might as well take off our shoes, for we are standing on holy ground. Just as Moses removed his shoes when he saw the miracle of a replenishing fire, so do we bare our feet as we prepare to bare all, sitting before our fiery box of miracles. We echo the psalms of former pilgrims and wonder whether their faint echo too might be heard at some point on our journey.

As we dive into the realm of cyberspace, God's inner life comes more clearly into focus the deeper we go.

"From the depths we call upon You, O God," says Ps. 130.

To those depths we now embark, O God, to find You.

I

The Death of "the Shepherd"

The Lord is my companion, nothing shall I lack.

—Ps. 23:1 (alternative translation)

All language about God must be analogical. . . . The fact is that all language about everything is analogical; we think in a series of metaphors.

—Dorothy L. Sayers, *The Mind of the Maker*

I first connected to the Internet late in the summer of 1995. I had just hooked up a new computer in my home and was playing around with this new supernatural toy when suddenly I was in what they call a chat room. I looked up at the top of an almost-blank screen and saw that there were only two names there, and one of them was me. Well, not really me, but my screen name. Hamrab.

The other person was called Whalermouth. I tried to figure out what that meant, but then figured that if that other person was trying to do the same with my name he'd be having a hell of a time. It wasn't worth trying to shake the anonymity.

Then, my four-year-old son Ethan noticed some words on the screen. "Hello, Hamrab, tell me if you are there."

My God, it talks! The computer was talking to me. Or really, some completely unknown yet distinct person, created in God's image, just as all human beings are, yet totally unseen and unheard, was reaching out to me as a human being in this most inhuman of environments. What was I to do?

I wasn't ready for this. Do I answer? Do I let on that I'm really there? Well, I typed in, "Hamrab says hello." Totally flustered and not wanting to get involved with anyone who would call himself Whalermouth, I clicked my way out of the room and to a local weather report. It was an easy click, much easier than hanging up the phone on all those solicitors who call at dinnertime. It was too easy, in fact, because the human factor had been so masked by words on a screen. I'm not even sure why I said hello in the first place.

The fact that my son was there is not in itself significant, except that he had helped me to turn the thing on. You know someday, maybe when he's sixteen, he'll be able to hit a baseball farther than his old man. And someday, like maybe when he's ten, he'll be a few technological light-years ahead of me. But that's okay, because I know that my parents, when they were my age, were thrilled just to be able to manipulate the old rabbit ears to get decent black-and-white reception of Milton Berle. That was the extent of their technological prowess, back in those good old days when gophers were pesky animals, the net was what you caught flies in on a hot summer day, and the web was where Dad had to re-string his son's baseball glove.

But all that has changed in just a few short years.

And God has changed, too.

Well, God hasn't really changed, or at least I don't think so. What is changing is how we think of God, and the metaphors we use to describe Him . . . I mean Her . . . I mean, not God, but "spirituality." I mean, can you see how confusing it's getting?

Confusing it may be, but no more perplexing than the transformations taking place in how we look at the world around us and the language with which we express it. As we reconfigure our images of the sacred to fit our new era of technological interface, the results could be spiritually enriching for each of us, and of great benefit both to organized religion and to society at large. But in order for that upgrade to take place, we must switch our default from outmoded images of the sacred to something more user-friendly.

But before I lapse completely into cyberbabble, let me back up and state my case for reimagining God.

Over the centuries, people of all faiths have employed countless metaphors to describe that which is both Ultimate and ultimately indescribable. The Hebrew Bible alone contains dozens of different images of God, envisioning the sacred as everything from a male warrior to a mother eagle. Each of these represents not only a view of divinity, but also a way of looking at the world—and ourselves. Those who composed the book of Exodus' triumphant Song of the Sea, who called God a "Man of War," had a worldview that was decidedly patriarchal, where an active God with human features could take sides in wars against lesser gods and humans. It was a world where justice prevailed. At the other extreme we have Job, to whom God was a voice out of the whirlwind, distant, terrifying and beyond understanding, reflecting the unjust world in which the righteous Job suffered so horribly.

As each generation has struggled to understand its place in the cosmos, it has fashioned a God to facilitate that process. Some might claim that this process makes a mockery of Western religions, which typically see the fashioning of divine images as idolatrous behavior. But the second commandment, the one that says "Make no other Gods before me," says nothing about making other *metaphors*.[2] Idolatry is when you point to a rock and say, "That's God." When you point to the Grand Canyon and say, "My *God!*" you are not saying that the canyon *is* God, but that the awesome spectacle of that huge carved-out rock is helping you to *experience* God. We experience God in many different ways, whenever we sense awe or profound gratitude, order, serenity or wonder. As new technologies take hold, these transcendent feelings are evoked in new ways and become more commonplace and accessible. It is no surprise that the popularity of books, music and films with spiritual themes has increased markedly in recent years.

While the latter part of the twentieth century had no monopoly on turbulence—and it is true that through all of history the only constant has been change—the pace of change has increased dramatically over the past three decades. At least it feels that way. Some could claim that the first part of this century was even more tumultuous, what with the inventions of the airplane, automobile and modern mass warfare. But that is of little solace to so many today who feel so lost and detached, reeling with displacement.

Perhaps this alienation stems from organized religion's inability to keep up. In the past, religion has been at the forefront either of opposing change (as with the condemnation of "rebels" like Galileo and Spinoza), or promoting it (as with the eventual embrace of great religious figures like Paul and Isaiah). But right now we hear few powerful voices of faith and very little direction from the pulpit. Our clergy seem bent on clinging to old metaphors that have no relevance to people whose worldview has been altered radically. Our churches and synagogues seem curiously out of touch with how most of us are feeling about religion, to the point where many people have become far more comfortable not using the term *religion* at all, replacing it with the more generic word "spirituality." Yet religion is not dead, just as God was not really dead in the 1960s, despite all claims to the contrary. What is dead is the prime metaphor of God that sustained Americans throughout the middle of the twentieth century.

What's dead is "the Shepherd."

I can recall the one time I tried to use a new translation of the twenty-third Psalm at a funeral. Immediately afterwards, I was verbally decapitated by an angry mourner for turning the "Valley of the Shadow of Death" into the "Valley of Deepest Darkness" and for changing that cup that "runneth over" into one that "overflows." But my greatest transgression was to tamper with the prime metaphor of that seminal psalm. "The Shepherd" provided the key image of God that sustained American Christians and Jews through the horrors of the Great Depression and cataclysmic wars. That tranquil image of calm certainty allowed people to submit, to accept a lot that might easily include premature loss and tragedy, to resist despair in stoic confidence that right would triumph and that their side *was* right. The shepherd metaphor presented God as a loving (male) caretaker, not as intimate as a parent, nor as demanding as a teacher, king or judge. Americans were suffering, but the Shepherd was in complete control of our destinies and, most importantly, He was a God who took responsibility for us. Americans needed to believe that God had a stake in us.

So this was the one time that I changed "shepherd" to "companion," an alternative translation of the same Hebrew word. "The Lord is my Companion." Sounded good to me.

Big mistake.

That mourner, who not coincidentally came from that wartime generation, was looking for the soothing stroke of a shepherd's staff. The last thing he wanted at that moment was a "companion."

Since that day I've stayed with "shepherd" at funerals, but I've abandoned that metaphor in every other sense. For I have come to understand that precisely that which galvanized my parents' generation is now numbing my contemporaries and our children. The shepherd metaphor does not comfort me anymore, if it ever did. It has nothing to do with what provides me with the spiritual sustenance I need to make sense of my life. It simply doesn't resonate, for a number of reasons.

As a Jew, I cannot imagine myself in the role of sheep, especially when six million of my fellow Jews were led like sheep to the slaughter. Although many resisted and most were heroic even in passive resistance, the image of sheep-to-the-slaughter remains, nearly six decades later, the pervasive nightmare of the Jewish people. Sheep are passive, plump and witless sweaters-in-waiting. The idea of being a sheep sickens me.

As a human being, I can not trust a God who, on His shepherd's watch, would allow His sheep to die. The shepherd God might already have been on the critical list before World War II, with new technologies and urban sprawl already rendering this metaphor obsolete. But the Holocaust was the final blow. If the wolves eat the sheep, how can we not fire the shepherd?

As a pastor, I find the shepherd-flock image stifling to my ministry and to the congregation. New models of spiritual leadership placing the pastor in the role of a companion provide fertile ground for me. As a fellow seeker, I am able to lead by example, without prodding, with room for my own experimentation, with allowance for an occasional failure. I've found most pastors have great difficulty coming down from the pasture, but once they do the effect is liberating, for them and their former flock.

And finally, as a participant in the technological revolution currently changing the way we look at everything, I have found new metaphors that are much more appealing, new ways of organizing my universe that connect me to that which is Greater than myself.

So I've been searching for God online.

Incidentally, I also believe it's possible to find spirituality in my VCR instruction manual. And in my home videos, my cell phone, my beeper, my remote control, my cable box and television screen; in the Hubbell telescope and the space shuttle, in my microwave oven and in a cloned sheep called Dolly. How I see God in these other technological phenomena is the subject for a more broad-based book; yet in some sense, a deep search for God on the Internet, the subject of this study, is a microcosm of the larger issue.

Through my search for God online, I've discovered danger signals along the journey. I believe God can be found on the Internet, but God can also be lost there. In the end, I'll offer no conclusive answers, no lightning-bolt revelations, just lots of new insight gained from one man's spiritual struggle in front of a computer monitor.

Through this book, we'll explore together some new ways to find enlightenment in this technological age, not by rejecting the material world but rather by elevating it, so that it can elevate us. For me, there is no other choice but to seek

God through engagement in this world. I come from a tradition that refrains from asceticism. When the world seems to be going haywire, a Jew can't just run off and hide. Neither can we take technology and make it into yet another idol, as cult groups like Heaven's Gate have done. We are enjoined to grapple with the world and make it better, not to escape from it. Admittedly, there are some highly respected ascetic traditions, including some that have biblical roots, which do see great merit in solitude. But even the monastic life typically is not intended as an escape from material reality that surrounds it, but ultimately as a contributor to its salvation.

The death of the shepherd metaphor has brought with it the death of rugged individualism as the American ideal. For that shepherd was also, thinly disguised, the Marlboro man, the John Wayne general and the Humphrey Bogart cafe owner. The God of the past generation was a lonely sort, accepting His solitude because that's what true leadership was all about. During the Cold War, America had to stand tall in the saddle, rifle cocked, ready to ward off "evil" Indians and wolves. The God I sought and, to an extent, found on the Web is quite different, and so is the world that we live in. Today's God dances with wolves and prances with Pocahontas (at least with the Disney version). The age of individualism and Cold War wagon circling has given way to one of mystical outreach and interconnection. America's Declaration of Independence has been replaced, in a spiritual sense at least, with a more universal Declaration of Interdependence.

So now we escape the green pastures where our cup has run dry and venture boldly beyond the valley of the shadow of death, to explore the rocky terrain of our real and virtual universe, in search of the God we believe in.

2

The First Journey
Sacred Stones in Gentle Light

A Pilgrim's Diary: Dawn in Jerusalem

There are ten portions of beauty in the world. Nine are in Jerusalem, one in the rest of the world. There are ten portions of suffering in the world. Nine in Jerusalem and one in the rest of the world.

—Avot de Rabbi Natan
(ancient collection of rabbinic commentary)

I'm sitting before the screen, somewhere around ten at night. So where do I want to "God" today? It seems so strange using the Internet for a pilgrimage. I've become so accustomed to the utilitarian use of this technological tool. My typical nightly ritual involves checking email; corresponding with congregants, other friends and relatives; and checking out a few key Websites. Now I'm determined to plunge.

I call up the search engine AltaVista and punch in "pilgrimage"—46,510 Web pages are available to me. I decide to opt first for the most familiar, one I find among my bookmarked venues: Virtual Jerusalem, *www.virtual.co.il*, a site packed with Israeli and Jewish links. I know exactly where I want to begin, at a site I've visited many times before, a live shot of the Western Wall provided by Kotel Kam ("Kotel" being the Hebrew word for that sacred Wall). The camera, provided by a Yeshiva called Aish Hatorah, the "Flame of Torah," is located high above the back of the large plaza leading up to the ancient remains of the Second Temple.

It is just before dawn in Jerusalem as the picture unfolds onto my screen. The front half of the plaza and the Wall itself shimmer in light so bright that I almost need to shade my eyes, staring at it from six thousand miles away. The back of the plaza is in shadows.

While I assume that the light is artificial and that the sun has not yet risen, the contrast between shadow and light, always so dramatic in Jerusalem, is intensified by the emptiness of the plaza. Two black-garbed ultra-Orthodox Jews (*Haredim*) are praying individually next to the Wall, one at the far left-hand corner, another toward the middle. Two others are walking aimlessly in the vicinity. Otherwise, stone, light and shade are all there is. I've never seen the plaza so empty—so devoid of human distraction. The past few times I've visited the Wall in person, the often-nasty infighting between *Haredim* and more liberal Jews has diverted my attention from the ethereal allure of those stones. There have been occasions when my pilgrimage groups and I have been looked upon with suspicion, or worse. Not so this time. I'm invisible to the *Haredim*, an apparition glancing over their shoulders, taking my own possession of this sacred spot. I'm present in Jerusalem and I've never been so at peace in the presence of the Wall.

True, I'm not really there. But is God really there?

Is God actually sitting on those stones, in the guise of a dove, as a Jewish legend has it? Do those impassioned written pleas placed within its crevices have any better chance of reaching heaven than my own petitions from home? Does a God who is everywhere really reside more in those precincts that humans declare to be sacred? If not—and I believe not—then what makes those places sacred at all? Why do millions of people dream all their lives to visit a single place, oftentimes saving for years and spanning oceans to get there? In a few short hours, I'll visit several once-in-a-lifetime locations, and maybe I'll find out why. What my grandmother never got to see, and what my great-grandmother couldn't imagine ever seeing as she dreamed only of escaping Czarist persecution, I can now visit with a few clicks of the mouse. In the accelerated cyberworld, I can make a dozen once-in-a-lifetime pilgrimages in a single evening, and truly be present at each.

I am really there because my complete attention is devoted to being there. Similarly, I could "be there" with the help of a photo in lieu of a computer screen; or by a Hebrew prayer hung along my eastern wall (east being the direction of Jerusalem). This contemplative tool, known as the *Mizrach* (meaning "east"), has for centuries helped Jews in the Diaspora to focus their hopes on Jerusalem. Now the Kotel Kam is doing the same thing, only the picture is live, and it is stunning. Looking at it makes me mindful of it and therefore "there."

God is "there," too, in the same way. But God is simultaneously here as well, in my darkened study in the United States, as I tap and click silently and intently while my kids sleep across the hall. God is in this machine, too. To paraphrase the Kotzker Rebbe, God is wherever people let God in.

In Judaism, God is "portable"

3

Belief and Bytes: Can God and Technology Get Along?

The most miraculous thing is happening. The physicists are getting down to the nitty-gritty, they've really just about pared things down to the ultimate details, and the last thing they ever expected to happen is happening. God is showing through.

—John Updike, *Roger's Version*

*B*efore we open up a home computer for the first time, it always pays to look at the instructions. If you are like me, you peruse the diagrams for about twenty minutes, determined at first to go it alone. But then reality sets in— that same feeling people have when diapering a child for the first time, when we realize, "My God, if I do this wrong, I could screw up the kid for life!" The fear of making The Big One is so pervasive that within an hour either you've called tech support or your best friend the computer whiz and asked him or her to come over. The desire for simplicity and infallibility leads us to select computer hardware and software based not on the quality of the product, but on how "user-friendly" it claims to be. One company, recognizing that need, promised in advertisements that the assembly of its computer would be an "out-of-box experience."

If only life itself could be an "out-of-box experience."

So now that we are about to open up our technological marvels to look for God, it pays to take a quick look at our "user-friendly" assembly chart, even if some of it happens to be in ancient Hebrew. If we are to figure out how God has been installed somewhere in our hard drive, or in our VCR or microwave, we first need to have an inkling as to what it is exactly that we are looking for. Seeking God is a complicated business; finding God, however, is astoundingly simple—once we are in proper seeking mode. How do we find God anywhere, inside or outside of the computer frame?

What We Say *Here* Is Heard *There*

There is an additional preliminary question that we must confront before proceeding on this journey, even before we open the box and take our first look at the instructions: Why should we be on this journey at all? Why look for God in modern technological devices? After all, haven't our preachers been telling us for centuries that technology is the work of the devil? Aren't machines the antithesis of God, draining our lives of whatever human qualities that might still remain? *From the religious perspective, isn't technology evil?*

The answer is yes. And no. One major presupposition I bring to this book is that technology is inherently neutral, with the capacity to produce both good and evil. The microchip is no different in that sense from the first fire created by cave-people; and it is productive to use the analogy of fire here. Fire has the capacity to be an instrument both of creation and of cataclysmic destruction, often simultaneously. When we think of forest fires started by humans, whether planned or accidental, which destroy acres of trees but also allow young saplings to grow unimpeded, we can see both the raw creative and destructive power of technology. It is not the fire that creates and destroys, however, but the person who holds that power in his or her hand.

Technology, from the Greek *technologia*, meaning "the systematic treatment of an art or craft," is defined by the *American Heritage Dictionary* as: *the application of science, especially to industrial or commercial objectives.* If we see technology as exactly that, a tool, we can begin to understand why even pious religious leaders were not afraid of technological advances, and why Rabbi Avraham Yaakov of Sadigora said this about a century ago:

> *You can learn something from everything:*
>
> *From the railways we learn that one moment's delay can throw everything off schedule.*
>
> *From the telegraph we learn that every word counts.*
>
> *And from the telephone, that what we say Here is heard There.*[3]

It certainly is easy to blame technology for the ills we see in society today. Thanks to the wonders of the technological mind, we are capable of destroying the world many times over through nuclear weapons; and if that doesn't work, we can destroy immense populations in a few instants with biological and chemical weapons. If all else fails and we actually survive the missiles, our technological society has given us enough acid rain and fluorocarbons to destroy our water and atmosphere. If we didn't heed these warnings, the history of the past century should be enough evidence to convince us to be most wary of technology. Before the twentieth century we had bloody wars, but the primary victims of those encounters were soldiers on the battlefields. The twentieth century brought mass destruction of civilian populations in heretofore unheard-of dimensions. Rabbi Avraham Yaakov

might have had much to learn from the train, but what civi-
lized person today can even think of a train—or an oven—
without eventually thinking of Auschwitz? And it is very
difficult to contemplate the wonders of rocketry without
invoking grim memories of the blitzkrieg over London. The
phone might have been a marvel, but it has paved the way
for wiretapping and the loss of privacy—Big Brother would
have been inconceivable before the twentieth century. Technology has some gruesome baggage to overcome.

Techno-God *Versus* Nature-God

The debate about technology came to a head in the
1960s, when the heart-thumping race to the moon coincided
with the technological nightmare of Vietnam. For some, it
seemed as if God had created us and given us fire for the
specific purpose of conquering the galaxy. But for others,
the fire of napalm and burning bodies left an indelible mark.
For some, technology was the source of all good; for others,
it could bring only evil.

Either side, pro- or anti-technology, could point to the Bible
for support. In fact, they could point to two stories in the
same book, just one chapter apart. In fact, these two stories
are the same story. They are the two Creation accounts.

Most people see the six-day Creation story found in Gen.
1 as the only version, but that's not what we read in the text.
After the end of that account and institution of the first
Sabbath, it is as if God starts over again, beginning in
chapter 2, verse 4: "These are the products of heaven and
earth when they were created, on the day that God made
earth and heaven. . . ." The two Creation stories contrast in

many ways: The second is earth-centered, with the first focusing much more on the heavens. It is noteworthy that the first begins, "In the beginning God created the heavens and the earth," while the second commences that way and then, apparently intentionally, reverses that order, with earth taking precedence over the heavens.

If the second Creation story were a movie, its opening shot would be of a dry, parched field suddenly brought to life by misty geysers of water. Once those geysers have saturated the meadow, the camera might pan around to reveal a steamy, primitive Woodstock, complete with naked humans. The first creation story, better known to most of us, would likely begin with total darkness, then a tennis-ball–sized earth would slowly rise over the horizon, much as it did for the astronauts of Apollo 8, when they became the first human beings to orbit the moon. On that Christmas Eve, 1968, that first earthrise was greeted with—what else?—the words of Gen. 1.

In Gen. 1, God speaks and light appears, the waters separate from the land and heavenly orbs appear. In Gen. 2, God does not issue commands. God plants. God waters. God grows vegetation. In Gen. 1, God is a master planner and analytic mind of the first order, able to break down complex problems and create by giving orders and making distinctions. It is creation through separation: heaven from earth, light from dark, firmament from water, water from land, day from night. In Gen. 2, God is a farmer, a nurturing hand, a more passive but caring observer. The passive tense is used often here (e.g., "God caused trees to sprout"). The second Creation account is organic.

What is most pertinent to our discussion is the role of the

human beings in each account. The two Creations yield two very different views of human nature and responsibility. Rabbi Joseph Soloveichik, among others, has documented this in his interpretive writings.[4] In the first, man and woman are created simultaneously on the sixth day, and created in God's image. There are many ambiguities in the verses describing their creation (Gen. 1:26–30), but God's command to the first couple is absolutely clear: "Be fruitful and multiply, fill the earth and subdue it; and rule over the fish of the sea, the bird of the sky, and every living thing that moves on earth."

In modern parlance, we could imagine the same God instructing us, "I've given you fire; it is My special gift to you. You may use it to dominate all of creation, on land, in space, in the sea. And the same goes for computer technology and telecommunications and modern medicine, too. Clone all you want, for all I care! And check out the moon ASAP—it'll be a giant leap for mankind. My universe is yours to conquer."

The second account has an entirely different view of man and woman. Here they have names, Adam and Eve. Adam comes before Eve, and isn't so much created as birthed, by God. God breathes life into his lifeless clay, and later, from that same clay, God completes the creation of humanity by forming Eve from Adam's side. Adam and Eve aren't given license to subdue nature here, but rather to establish a relationship with nature through the act of naming.

With these dual Creation accounts, the Bible seems to be both endorsing technological advance and suggesting a more natural course eschewing the subduing. It would be easy to simplify matters and say that Gen. 1 is pro-technology and

Gen. 2 pro-nature and opposed to technological manipulation of our resources. Too easy. The question is, why does the Bible give us both? So that we might choose between them, or so that we might synthesize them? That for me is the not-so-hidden message of the dual Creation accounts: *Technological conquest is divinely desired, but only if it results in the enhancement of relationship.* If technology is essentially a neutral tool, like fire, such a positive outcome is possible, in spite of the gas chambers and ovens, in spite of napalm and nukes.

But many don't agree. Especially in the aforementioned 1960s, assorted authors lined up to condemn what some in previous decades had naively called "the March of Progress." Octavio Paz, the Mexican poet, wrote in 1967, "The nihilism of technology lies not only in the fact that it is the most perfect expression of the will to power . . . but also in that it lacks meaning."[5]

And Archibald MacLeish, in a 1968 article from *Saturday Review,* put in prose the alienation that so many were feeling:

> *Wilderness and silence disappeared from the countryside, sweetness fell from the air, not because anyone wished them to vanish or fall but because throughways had to floor the meadows with cement to carry the automobiles which advancing technology produced.*[6]

Everywhere things seemed to be falling apart. Songwriters like Tom Lehrer looked around at our smoggy cities and mused about how we might all soon be wearing gas masks, and that breathing would be fine—until we inhale.

But the joke couldn't hide the growing fear that our air was unbreathable and our water undrinkable.[7]

Technology began to make a comeback among the counterculture set in the mid-1970s. With the Vietnam and Apollo paradigms beginning to fade into history and the computer age about to begin, people settled into a brief hiatus where technology could be evaluated with sober appreciation and guarded apprehension.

It wasn't the TV or jet plane or superhighway that was destroying modern life, it's how these devices, in the true spirit of the divide-and-conquer first Creation account, had been used to subdue nature rather than to promote relationship.

Now, with the computer age upon us, there is no escaping the power and almost hypnotic tug of what many are beginning to again call "progress." We must be careful not to embrace the whole, when every innovation still contains the seeds of potential destruction. But neither should we fear it. For these postmodern marvels are no more and no less than extensions of ourselves: Telephones are our extended mouths and ears, the automobile our extended legs, the television our extended eyes and the computer our extended brain. What Marshall McLuhan wrote in 1964 is even more evident today:

> *The medium is the message. This is merely to say that the personal and social consequences of any medium—that is, any extension of ourselves—result from the new scale that is introduced into our affairs by each extension of ourselves, or by any new technology.*[8]

We can now see farther than any human eye has ever seen: It is miraculous, but it is still our eye that is seeing. We can now communicate instantly with people orbiting the moon: Amazing, but it is our natural eardrums vibrating when we hear them quote Gen. 1. A computer can beat a human being in chess: Remarkable, but no matter who wins, it is a triumph of human daring and ingenuity. The human side of the story hasn't changed since Adam and Eve, but the scale has changed dramatically.

This reality was driven home to millions of Americans in May 1998, when a malfunctioning satellite suddenly pulled the plug on 80 percent of the nation's almost 50 million pagers. Havoc reigned, but primarily because of the human implications that are as old as creation. The *New York Times* quoted one woman, a wireless communications analyst named Suzanne Stein, who had paged her husband four times to ask what he wanted her to pick up for dinner. "I was so angry that he didn't return my call that it was like, 'I'm going to divorce you if you don't page me back right now.'"[9] What we have here is a failure to communicate—much as God, Adam and Eve had in the Garden of Eden, when Eve told the serpent that she wasn't supposed to *touch* the forbidden fruit when in fact God has instructed her merely not to *eat* it. She touched it. She was okay. So she ate it.

While we might bemoan our sudden dependence on technological devices like pagers to get our word across, how different is that from the book of Numbers, where God instructs Moses to speak to a rock in order to draw water from it, and Moses screws up the message and hits the rock instead? What we have here is a failure to communicate.

God's Pager

If we look at Num. 19, we see no pagers or satellites, but we see Moses standing with his brother Aaron in what was for them Mission Control. The "Tent of Meeting," as it was called, or *Ohel Moed* in Hebrew, has been compared to a giant divine transmitter by off-target theorists who presuppose the involvement of extraterrestrials in biblical events. While I don't subscribe to those theories, the Bible itself sees this *Ohel Moed* as the place where the divine intent could be ascertained with greatest clarity, where God's glory was made manifest. That happens here, and although the divine message is delivered with digital clarity, Moses still gets it wrong. Fittingly, God's charge to Moses is to communicate—to speak—and Moses lacks that ability at that time. Speaking was never his forte to begin with, but in spite of his speech impediment, he was always able to communicate with his enemies, his friends and his God. Suddenly and inexplicably (except possibly for the excuse of his having just buried his sister Miriam), this all breaks down. Moses reacts in anger toward his people, calling them "bitter rebels," and he simultaneously disobeys his God. When communications break down among human beings, a sacred bond is severed, and God no longer resides between the parties as the promoter of love and relationship.

That's why Moses' punishment was so severe. People often wonder how one seemingly small slipup such as that could have caused Moses to be denied the chance to lead his people into the Promised Land. But that was no small slipup at all. For what Moses had done was to sever the satellite link between God and the people. In many ways, he was that link, and the Tent of Meeting, restricted to so few, was the place where God communicated with utter clarity. When Moses miscommunicated the divine intent, the people were left with plenty of water to drink, but with a spiritual alienation that could never be quenched. "Hear O Israel, the Lord our God, the Lord is One," is what we are told in Deut. 6. If people are to come to *know* God, the first thing we must be able to do is *hear* God.

We need to find God in our pagers.[10] We also need to see how technology impedes our quest for spiritual enlightenment. The haywire satellite nearly severed marriages. On the other hand, the great blackout of 1965 resulted in a record number of births exactly nine months later. Colossal blizzards, which bury decades of "progress" under feet of snow, have had similar life-enhancing effects. What shines through it all is the human factor.

Which means that our task of finding God's place in all of this is not only an intellectual curiosity, it is a basic human necessity. If we are to maintain our humanity through these years of explosive change, we must seek out the divine image. We can do this without foreboding, because God is there to be found; all we need to do is look. It is like the story of a group of children playing hide-and-seek. One boy hides and waits for his friends to find him, but to no avail. Hours pass, and still no one comes. Finally he goes home and cries to his mother, "Why is it that no one came to look for me?" His mother responds, "That must be exactly how God feels. God is hidden, but so close to us; yet how few of us seek God out. How lonely it must be to be God."

If we look for God only in the usual places, we are sure to miss the mark. It is only when we seek God outside the sanctuary and beyond the prayer book that we have the best chance of succeeding. And technology is the terrain we all inhabit right now.[11] That's where the path of our searching must lead. Pope Pius XII said it in his Christmas message in 1953, and these words resonate even more today: "The Church welcomes technological progress and receives it with love, for it is an indubitable fact that technological progress comes from God and, therefore, can and must lead to Him."

4

The First Journey
Sacred Stones in Gentle Light

Jihad and the Flames of Torah

As for the view of Jerusalem from afar, filled with
brilliance and beauty, it is one of the famous
wonders. . . . When God grants the pilgrim the
favor of arriving at the solemn al-Aqsa shrine and
the prayer station venerated by Abraham, he
experiences an indescribable feeling of joy and
well-being and forgets the pains and troubles he
has endured.

—Mujir al-Din, fifteenth century Moslem historian, who lived in Jerusalem
most of his life, yet the sight of the city still evoked in him tremendous awe

*T*hey let God in quite a bit in Mecca, so I want to go there next.

They let God in, but they would never let me in. As a Jew, I'd have a tough time getting into the entire country of Saudi Arabia, much less making it to Islam's most sacred city. But with the Internet, it's a breeze to get past the guards. If the gatekeepers of the Kotel couldn't keep me at bay, I should have no problem with Mecca. So I click onto *www.islam.org*, and instantly I'm staring at a bustling souk of Moslem educational and religious information and links. A headline asks, "How can I spread Islam?" They are assuming I am Moslem. Am I the only Jew ever to enter this site? Of course, there is no way of knowing, nor is there any way of their knowing (I think), so I'm emboldened to go further.

My pilgrimage to Mecca takes me past several Islamic links, including the "Jihader's Islamic Web Page" *(www.geocities.com/Athens/Delphi/ 9215)*. I click and what unfolds before me is not Mecca at all, but a return ticket to Jerusalem [a more recent visit of the site indeed shows a photo of the Ka'ba in Saudi Arabia on its main page]. I see on the top third of the screen a fabulous vista of the Old City, with the Dome of the Rock at its center; this is an extension of the same view I had just seen of the Temple Mount, but quite literally from the other side, the perspective of Kotel Kam's twin brother. The view is a classic picture-postcard panorama, taken from the Mount of Olives just after sunrise, when, as one gazes from its eastern edge, the city is painted a shimmering gold by the bright desert sun. Inscribed above that photo is a phrase in Arabic, then beneath it the translation, "In the name of Allah, Most gracious, most merciful." On my way to Mecca, something is pulling me back toward Jerusalem, but an inverted Jerusalem. It is a view I've often seen but this time I'm seeing it from eyes through which I would never look: Jerusalem—Islam's third holiest city.

I think of all the stereotypes this Jew and this American has grown to accept: Islam equals violence, terror and vengeance. Judaism equals love and compassion. But what is my initial Web-dive revealing to me? A live view of the Jewish sacred place is provided by the burning "flames of Torah," and Islam's perspective of the same place is associated with the "most merciful." Justice and mercy, passion and serenity are balanced in two early-morning shots of the same holy mountain, but mercy is mentioned on the Islamic side, and the flames of passion from the Jewish. There is confusion here, but not one that leads to despair, rather one that links the two views of the same place in a sublime balance.

Since I've stumbled upon a site dedicated to *Jihad*, I click to discover what that controversial concept is all about. I scroll down a lengthy description emphasizing that what is often mistranslated as "holy war" has everything to do with holiness and little to do with war. One can live and die for a supreme cause without having to be engaged in military activity. While there are wars that are indeed *Jihads*, I am impressed with the definition offered here, "The best form of *Jihad* is a declaration of the truth in front of a despotic ruler." *Jihad* is less a declaration of war than a passionate commitment to leading a holy life.

And it is holy not only in deed but also in intent. Mohammed is quoted here as saying, "Actions are but intentions." According to the site, this means, "the value of any action is determined by intention behind it and the purpose for which it is done." In Judaism, by contrast, action tends to take precedence over intent, although there is a desire for intention too, which Jews call *Kavanah*. Without it, the act of prayer is nothing but a rote recital of meaningless passages. With it, prayer becomes a gateway to a life of holiness. No religion can survive without a careful balance between passion and action. If there were no set times for prayer, we would pray only when "in the mood," and judging from the weekly attendance at most places of worship I know, most people are not "in the mood" that often.

Prayer . . . I click a few times and look at the times for Moslem prayer times for my geographic location. A couple more clicks and I see on my screen the Jewish prayer times for the same place and day. Moslems pray five times daily, Jews, three. Moslems' lives appear even more regulated by prescribed action, yet they speak of intent as their highest value.

Actions are but intentions. . . . I've never looked at the possibility of synthesizing the two, as Moslems seem to almost effortlessly. I'm beginning to feel pangs of what has been called "sacred envy," the feeling that another faith or denomination has something desirable that mine doesn't. I know it's not that simple, that Jewish history is filled with champions of pure faith, people able to achieve that magical synthesis. For Islam, Judaism and other faiths, the embodiment of such pure faith is the martyr, who is willing to die for his or her beliefs; for a martyr, the ultimate action is also a supreme gesture of faith.

I pull back from the screen. Do I really see martyrdom as my ideal gesture of faith? Should I? Does God want me to live with such selfless devotion, such complete submission? A willingness to die? For what?

For Judaism?

For God?

Whose God?

My people pray to that God at specific times daily, times that overlap almost exactly those times when Moslems are praying to the same God with a fervor that we all believe God wishes of us.

And when are Moslems allowed to begin reciting their daily prayers? I check it out, clicking away to another site and read that *Fajr*, earliest prayers can begin just before dawn, when "a column of whiteness rises upwards from the east."

I reflect on that live shot from the Western Wall, the pre-dawn whiteness of the illumined stones and the *Haredim* at prayer. At dawn, when what has been dark comes to first light, when colors first appear and dreams dissolve into reality; at dawn, when Jacob's mysterious, sacred stranger took quick leave of him following a night of incessant wrestling, when years earlier, Jacob woke from his dream and realized that God's presence was tangible . . . I am beginning to see a growing connection between my search for God and these delicate, early lights.

The internal logic of seeking God online is beginning to unfold before my eyes.

5

Where Do We Look for God?

When God set forth to create the universe, His
thought encompassed all the worlds at once. . . .
All were created in a single instant.

—Zohar, thirteenth century kabbalistic work

The world, you see, is like a drum; there is a Being
who plays all kinds of tunes on it.

—Ananda Moyi, contemporary Hindu writer

So, as we search for God online, what exactly are we looking for and where do we find it?[12]

1. We are looking for God in *relationship*. Martin Buber is the modern philosopher best known for the idea that God exists not so much within or above us but *between* us. Where there is relationship, where there is love and commitment, there is God. Of course, Buber didn't invent the idea. It is found throughout scripture, in relationships between humans and between people and God. A verse from First Samuel 20 could have come right out of Buber, where Saul's son Jonathan seals his dangerous friendship with David with the line, "God shall be *between* you and me, and between our offspring, forever." So wherever relationship is enhanced, we are on the proper trail, leading to God.

2. We experience God where there is *integration and wholeness*. The fundamental premise of most major world religions is that God is One. Granted, different religions get there in different ways, but even traditions that appear to be polytheistic strive for an underlying unity. But it is not unity alone that we seek when we look for God. Unity is bland. Unity implies sameness

and denies the uniqueness of each individual. What we seek is *interconnectedness*, in other words, oh my gosh here it comes, something that looks just like a spider's, er, well, a *web*. Have we heard that metaphor anywhere else?

Other metaphors for God demonstrate such integration. The modern Jewish philosopher Richard Rubenstein wrote in 1970,

> God is the ocean and we are the waves. In some sense each wave has its moment in which it is distinguishable as a somewhat separate entity. Nevertheless, no wave is entirely distinct from the ocean which is its substantial ground. The waves are the surface manifestations of the ocean. Our knowledge of the ocean is largely dependent on the way it manifests itself in the waves.[13]

The more we are integrated into the, uh, *web* of life without losing our uniqueness, the closer we come to experiencing divine bliss. That verse from Deut. 6 that has long been the Jewish credo, known in Hebrew as the *Sh'ma*, states this as both a definition and a challenge: "Hear O Israel, the Lord God, the Lord is One." That which we seek, which we also call God, is a state of absolute connection with the universe. What is inside us is also outside us. When we call out, we are answered; when we reach out, we are touched.

In fact, the ancient rabbis defined heaven in terms of this interconnection. Hell and heaven are absolutely the same, they said, with one small difference. In both places, people are seated around one long table, with a delicious meal in front of them. And in both places their elbows are locked straight and cannot be bent. In hell, those poor souls struggle mightily to feed themselves but can't reach their mouths with their forks. In heaven, each person feeds his neighbor and everyone eats and is satisfied.

An integrated universe is one where there is the constant hum of response, a world where what we say *here* is heard *there*. What we strive for in our search for the bonds of community and fulfilling love relationships is a little slice of heaven. A constant critique of technology is that it breaks such connections, that it atomizes people, separating them from one another and from their true selves. That tendency can be found and is not to be taken lightly. It must be tested again and again as we proceed.

3. We experience God where we sense order amidst chaos, when we are *secure.* This can occur in a variety of settings, within family and community, or alone. For a child this feeling can be evoked as simply as by cuddling up in bed with a parent during a storm, or by grasping a security blanket. For adults, security is much more elusive.

4. The divine is sensed when we encounter *amazement and awe,* what theologian Rudolph Otto called "mysterium" and "tremendum." This can be the result of a sensual or aesthetic experience or more intellectual encounter, say with a text, or the act of creation.

5. The divine experience can be an *act of emulation* of divine attributes, or as lovers of Latin like to call it,

Imitatio Dei. Since we are created in God's image, God's inclination toward both justice and compassion echoes in our own. And when we create works of profound beauty, we bathe ourselves in the divine creative impulse.

6. Finally, and this by no means exhausts all possibilities, we experience God when we become *fully human, embracing and enhancing life.* It is at those most poignant human moments, when a parent gives his or her child away at a wedding, or when a community envelops a mourner with compassion, that the divine and human intersect. In the words of Buber, "Man cannot approach the divine by reaching beyond the human; to become human is what this individual man was created for." Rabbi Irving (Yitz) Greenberg sees God's design and humanity's mission as advancing the "triumph of life" over death.[14] Any time we overcome despair, hopelessness or alienation, life triumphs and God is made present.

This in a nutshell is what we are looking for: a Source for that which enhances life, connects us to an orderly creation, makes us whole, makes us moral, amazes us, lifts us to a higher realm, makes us absolutely and fully human.

False Gods

And what aren't we looking for? Aside from the dated shepherd image described earlier, here are some of the caricatures of God that we all recognize, ones that reduce the Ineffable to a not-so-supreme being with a mean streak and a George Burns cigar.

Religion has been given a bad name by the likes of so-called religious leaders who are actually frauds, and by so-called skeptics who distort the religious message to their own nihilistic ends. The result is that we end up with an ungodly mess that few serious-minded seekers could consider seeking. We end up with, for example, the *Gotcha God.* This is the God who is there, who is watching and who's "gonna get ya."

A few years back I was alerted to the destructive potential of the Gotcha God by a "Far Side" cartoon and an article in the journal *Christian Century.* The cartoon depicts five people in a restaurant looking in horror toward the men's room. An embarrassed user of the room is emerging while a bell clangs and an illuminated sign reads, "DIDN'T WASH HANDS!" The article in *Christian Century* spoke of a survey conducted with the help of hidden cameras in washrooms, which discovered that about 80 percent of people washed their hands if someone else was in sight, but if no one was in sight 80 percent did not wash their hands.

It is no surprise that so many of us wash our hands—and pay our taxes, for that matter—only when we think someone is watching, and that we act very differently when we think no one is watching. It all stems from two phenomena: (1) the widespread inculcation of a Gotcha God and (2) the fact that we don't believe in it anymore. Even the shepherd metaphor retains more power.

The Gotcha God has lost its power. Whether or not people were reared on the idea that God is watching everything we do, few of us believe God will do anything about it. After the Holocaust, it is hard to imagine God punishing me for feeding my brussels sprouts to the dog under the table.

People don't mind their manners because of Gotcha God, even if they may have a few generations ago. Now, by far the greatest policemen of morality aren't divine authorities but children. When children enter a room, suddenly all swearing stops, people give charity, fasten seat belts, eat their brussels sprouts and wash their hands. For the sake of the children, adults become better people. But again, it's not because we want to be good, it's because someone is watching.

It's time to discard the Gotcha God. Any metaphor that has no power to help us become good and moral people is not one we should be teaching ourselves or others.

It's also time to do away with *God-on-High,* who answers prayers with aplomb, but only if you've been good. This God-on-High also has a mean streak, inflicting punishment and ruling wrathfully from a heavenly throne. That image is essentially infantile and stifling. It may have had its day, but for all intents that day ended between 1933 and 1945. We depend on God-on-High as a crutch, but it leaves many people incredulous. The Gotcha God and God-on-High were effectively refuted by the book of Job over twenty centuries ago. To their credit, these images have had staying power. But if we are to search for a divine presence that can respond to our deepest needs, we must go far beyond the kind of God who will give me an A on my history exam if I am good, but will then turn around and slaughter millions of innocent Bosnians.

A modern scholar of Jewish mysticism named Daniel Matt recently wrote a fascinating book entitled *God and the Big Bang.*[15] He brings us to a different understanding of divinity, one based on Jewish mysticism (kabbalah), but with ties to mystical traditions of other faiths as well. His view, although based on an age-old tradition, is strikingly apt for modern ears. Using the increasingly resonant metaphor of God as an ocean and each of us a wave, he says that it is a Oneness with God that we seek, not knowledge of or favor from a distant God far above us. Using the tools of Kabbalistic numerology, the Hebrew words for One *(Echad)* and for Love *(Ahavah)* have equal numeric value (thirteen). Add them together and you get twenty-six, the numerical value of the Hebrew divine name, *Y-H-V-H*. To be spiritual, then, is to cultivate an appreciation of Oneness and be open to the possibility of Love.

We live in a shattered world, where separation endures. But whenever we forge connections, we sense that mystery unfolding. When we are reunited with loved ones, we feel a pull that cannot be explained. I was in Israel for two weeks in the summer of 1997, and by the journey's end, I was ecstatic beyond words to be reunited with my family. I felt God's presence in that reunion. When we are enraptured by a lover's touch, or a sunset, when we look at a sacred text and discover to our wonder that it was speaking to us all along, this is where we find God. God is not *up there*. She is right here, in the bark of a tree, in a friend's voice, in a stranger's eye, both within us and beyond us. And between us.

In Daniel Matt's words, the Big Bang didn't happen somewhere out there, outside of us. Rather, we began inside the Big Bang; we now embody its primordial energy. With no cosmic parent watching over us, we have to care all the more for one another. When we speak of belief, it is a trust that we are part of something greater, integrated into a web of existence that is constantly evolving and expanding. When

I hear God, it is through the still, small voice of conscience; when I see God, it is in your eyes.

So now we know that we are looking for a different divine image. We also understand that this redefined God exists everywhere, and that it is incumbent upon us to seek God out, even to the farthest reaches of cyberspace.

6

The First Journey
Sacred Stones in Gentle Light

Mecca, Without Camels

Have they not traveled in the land that they should
have hearts with which to understand, or ears
with which to hear?

—Quran 22:46

*T*ime to move on, to Mecca, found at *www.sesrtcic.org*, and there I view the al-Haram mosque, called by the site "the web of Islamic pilgrimage," bathed in what looks like the white lights of early dawn. The angle of the photo is from on-high, much like that of the Dome of the Rock and the Western Wall in the Jerusalem shots. I don't know where the photographer is standing—I've never been to Mecca . . . until now. I am an invisible pilgrim, welcome in cyberreality where I would be most unwelcome in the other real life.

"Allah is the reality, it is He who gives life to the dead, who has power over all things," I read in Sura 22 of the Quran, the chapter that speaks of pilgrimage. It proclaims that the Sacred Mosque has been "made open to all men—equal is the dweller there and the visitor from the country." The Sura continues, "Proclaim the Pilgrimage (*hajj*) among men: they will come to thee on foot and on every kind of camel, emaciated on account of journeys through deep and distant mountain highways. That they may witness the benefits provided for them and celebrate the name of Allah."

Camels . . . mountain highways . . . I wonder whether clicking counts. Laying aside the question as to whether I'd be welcome for this cybervisit, I begin to wonder whether the manner of transportation is so crucial to the journey that only specific modes are allowable. Is fatigue a prerequisite for pilgrimage? I know how tired I am when I land in Israel, normally after a flight of at least ten hours. Without the stubble and sweat, I would almost feel as if I hadn't earned the privilege of ascending God's holy mountain. Perhaps that's why there is so much strife in Jerusalem. The people who actually live there can't possibly appreciate the difficulty of getting there, and thus they lose a large part of the special feeling of being in a sacred place. If they had to take a ten-hour flight each day to see those golden stones, no one would complain about traffic and dung; there would be no turf wars. There would be only the shuffle of barefooted pilgrims alighting from their camels and cabs.

Although on the Web one can not approximate the difficulty of the journey, one can still feel the wonder of arrival, made even more precious because the visit is so short.

For I must move on.

Computer time is measured not in footsteps but in lightning-quick flashes. From God's perspective, a human life is measured in such flashes. The sheer potential for speed moves us along. I can't dwell in Mecca; I've done it. Been there. If God is everywhere, and I seek God, so must I be everywhere. And now I can be.

I've reached Mecca, which was the goal. Next time, I'll complete their *Hajj*. For now I must complete my own.

7

The Cybervillage

*A*ll real living is meeting.

—Martin Buber, *I and Thou*

*N*ext time you surf the Web, check out my synagogue's Website at *www.tbe.org.*

You'll find there what you'll now find in thousands of other sites, for religious institutions, businesses, government organizations and individuals: a virtual Main Street. When you come to the Temple Beth El Website, you'll hear Jewish music and see a group of happy silhouetted figures dancing in a circle. Under the "Welcome to Beth El" sign, you'll see our motto, "A Jewish Village"; a place to sign in, so everyone will know your name; and lots of rooms to "visit," from the sanctuary to the religious school to, yes, even the rabbi's study. In the old days, a visit to the rabbi's study was usually not good news. For a child, it often meant that the offender had thrown one too many spitballs at a harried teacher or had verbally linked God to a bodily function. For an adult, the visit to that study occurred mostly at those most troubling of times, following a death in the family, or when confronting a deep spiritual crisis. Even more than the sanctuary, the rabbi's study was the inner sanctum, a place of dark mystery and trepidation.

Well, click that mouse and c'mon in!

A single click brings you to "The Rabbi's Study," and I'm there to greet you, bearing a personal message, a warm welcome, and a selection of my sermons and articles for you to read. We can have a conversation about my sermons, because you can email me instantly. Another quick click and you can see my picture, read my bio and see what I've been up to lately. And you can feel completely free to wander around my study because I'm not really there. And neither are you. Or are we?

Leaving that question aside for a moment, here's what you'll read upon entering my study:

> *Welcome to our Jewish Cybervillage! As our lives become increasingly harried, communication becomes more and more difficult. . . .*
>
> *But now we have the Internet, and with it, new hope. I believe that the Net has immense potential to bring people together, not as a replacement for real human contact but as a catalyst to it. . . . Congregants have had the chance to learn Torah, keep up with crucial news and temple happenings and begun to feel closer to one another through this technology. The village we've created online might be virtual, but the people behind these words are very real.*

On the face of it, the act of sitting in your home or office, alone, would be the least likely manner through which to find community. For the entirety of human history until very recently, the primary way to connect with other people was to be with them. Even when technology began to extend our voices, ears and vision—and the advent of radio and then television created our first virtual communities with presidential "fireside chats" and such—still the primary mode of human interaction through the mid-twentieth century was "in the flesh." In a landmark 1995 study of American social activity entitled "Bowling Alone," however, Robert D. Putnam saw a marked decrease in participation in civic involvement since the 1960s.[16] He viewed this as a sign of a breakdown in the fabric of American life and danger signal for democracy itself. Just as membership in organizations and bowling leagues has declined markedly, he observed, so has voter turnout, by nearly 25 percent in the past thirty years. Surveys indicate that every year since 1973, the number of Americans who report that "in the past year" they have attended a political rally or speech, served on a committee of some local organization or attended a public meeting on town or school affairs, has fallen precipitously. Putnam concluded, "by 1990, tens of millions of Americans had forsaken their parents' habitual readiness to engage in the simplest act of citizenship."

Putnam looked for the usual suspects to blame for this decrease in social involvement: mobility, the reduction of leisure time, then movement of women into the labor force, and, that most visible villain of all—technology. He observed the "privatization of leisure" as disrupting opportunities for human interaction.

What is of interest here is whether the Internet craze has advanced that trend, or reversed it. As I've mentioned, God is found primarily in relationship, not in isolation, and on the face of it, watching a computer screen is as isolating as watching a television screen. But the two are actually very different. Putnam's study predates our current obsession with Internet linkage. Over 20 million people worldwide are online at this moment, with 150,000 being added each month.[17] This number, recorded from a 1998 Internet guide, is already hopelessly out of date. Preliminary evidence is primarily anecdotal, but it indicates that this technological advance has at least a strong potential to bring real people together. On a Sunday in April 1998, I officiated at the wedding of two people who met online the previous New Year's eve, in an America Online (AOL) chat room.[18] The very next day, following a funeral, a congregant approached to thank me profusely for letting her know about it, so that she could be there for her close friend. How had she found out? She is one of approximately 160 congregants (of about 700 families) on my growing congregational email list. I had posted the notice the previous evening and she had read it that morning, about an hour before the event. Jewish funerals normally occur on the day following the death, often too soon for the newspapers or even the telephone "grapevine" to be of much use. But email was able to get her there. So on consecutive days, I experienced two major life-cycle events whose human content was enhanced by the Internet. God was more present at both events because of the simple act of people sitting alone in front of a computer monitor, typing in a few commands.

Something is at work here that needs to be investigated more fully. Something is happening to us. More and more people are telling me that the Internet has brought spirituality to their lives, and at the root of that feeling is the sense of real connection. We may now prefer to bowl alone, but we crave real community as much as our grandparents did; we're just not sure how to achieve it. That desire is, in my mind, biological and instinctive. Scientists have shown that even one-celled bacteria are capable of making the sacrifices necessary to organize into communities. It is a basic craving that all living organisms share, and the Internet seems to be satisfying it.

Virtual and Real

And the "virtual" world of the Internet has succeeded where "reality" has failed us. True, there is quite a bit on the Internet that one would have difficulty calling "spiritual" in nature: neo-Nazi conspiracies, hard and soft porn, banal personal home pages, really bad jokes, bogus journalism, unsubstantiated rumors run rampant and lots of weird stuff at just about every turn. This corresponds to my presupposition that technology is inherently neutral, with the capacity for good and evil, the sacred and the profane. That makes it much like your local bookstore, where you can pick up a Bible on one shelf and *Penthouse* a few aisles over. I can choose to make my reading experience at that store as spiritual as I want it to be. It depends where I decide to browse.[19]

And true, a recent study published in *American Psychologist* indicated that greater use of the Internet leads to increases in depression and loneliness.[20] The more people gravitate toward virtual communities, the study reported, the greater the sense of disconnection from vital day-to-day human contact. "A computer monitor can't give you a hug or laugh at your jokes," wrote a reporter for the American Psychological Association publication, *Monitor,* noting the antisocial consequences of the increased online socializing.

There will doubtless be more such studies over the coming

years as our cyberculture evolves, and they will likely be more positive. These negative preliminary findings are not especially surprising; new ideas are commonly upsetting to the contemporaneous social fabric. Telephones had a similarly negative impact on the amount of time spent relating with other people face-to-face, and look at what the automobile did for the urban, pedestrian culture of the horse-and-buggy era. Yet neither device would now be seen by most as antisocial and alienating. It takes time for society to catch up. However, just as society adapted to the car by inventing the suburban shopping mall and to the phone by inventing private lines for teenagers, civilization will soon adjust to the additional hours we spend socializing online.

One thing is certain: To the extent that the Internet is alienating, God cannot be found there, and the entire enterprise of seeking God there is an exercise in idolatry. For God to be found online, the experience must leave us more fully human and more fully connected to other real human beings.

Keyword: God

I checked one of the standard search engines, AltaVista, punched in "God" and found 3,920,476 matches on Websites alone. But that massive number only begins to scratch the surface of the spiritual potential of the Internet. When I joined the ranks of the "online" in 1995, one of my first stops was an AOL chat room on synagogue life. The question being discussed was why the majority of American Jews refuses to affiliate with a congregation. I perused about fifty responses, each one simultaneously disheartening and heartwarming. It was sad that so many felt so uncomfortable with organized religion, but very encouraging that at last they had a place, a religious fellowship of sorts, where they could share those concerns and connect.

Here is some of what I read:

> "When you walk into a (synagogue), one often feels as if one is being measured by one's knowledge. Non-observant? Yuck! Intermarried? Get lost!"

> "Cliques. Not much you can do here except find a few folks who are willing to greet strangers and try to make them feel welcome."

> "Your worth as a congregant is directly proportional to your financial contribution."

> "I'm president of a small NC temple. I feel there is an 'attitude' by some of the original members when welcoming new members. We are trying to change this now. Change takes time."

When I saw these remarks, coming from all over the map, from people of different ages and denominational affiliations, I realized that I was on to something big. I could relate to virtually every comment, as something that I and/or many of my own congregants had at times perceived about my synagogue. I felt as if I had tapped into a support group without walls.

8

The First Journey
Sacred Stones in Gentle Light

Madurai, Nataraja and the Dance

*W*hen you see the type of a nation's dance, you
know its character.

—Confucius

*T*he movement of whose body is the world, whose
speech is the sum of all language, whose jewels are
the moon and stars—to that pure Shiva I bow!

—*Abhinaya Darpana* (thirteenth century text
on the Barata Natya school of Indian dancing)

I look down the AltaVista–generated pilgrimage search list. It is a mixture of the sublime and the ridiculous, holy places abounding, and then there are house tours of the antebellum South and a "pilgrimage" of places venerated by fans of the Marx Brothers. After a quick refresher stop at a familiar place, the home page for United Synagogue Youth (U.S.Y.) Pilgrimage, the Israel experience of my denomination's youth groups, I turn my attention to number four on the AltaVista list: Madurai, in southern India, (www.incore.com/india/madurai.htm) advertised as "a center of learning and pilgrimage for centuries." The site seems interesting, but there is no photo of the Meenakshi temple, centerpiece of the sacred site. I read of the city's two-thousand-year history, involving what appear to be more conquests than any place this side of Jerusalem, including some time under Moslem rule. I learn that the city is named for the Pandyan king's daughter who, according to legend, was born with three breasts. At the time of her birth, the king was told that the extra breast would disappear when she met the man she was supposed to marry, and this happened when she met the Lord Shiva who later married her.

This form of breast reduction is news to me, so I store away the information, along with some questions. If Shiva could have an extra set of arms and legs—as many depictions show—why couldn't she hold on to her extra breast? But most of all, I ask myself why thousands of people make pilgrimage to this place every day, and where it fits into my own personal journey. It's worth checking out, so I call up the Meenakshi Temple's picture gallery at *www.madurai.com/gallery.htm.* Immediately I understand what lies behind the temple's popularity. The profusion of multicolored images of gods, goddesses, animals and mythical figures, decorating both the inside and outside of this high, intricate structure, are as detailed and ornate as the Western Wall is simple and stark. Where the Kotel bespeaks one, image-less deity, the Meenanshi invokes millions.

It is an avalanche to the eye.

Shiva is one of the patron gods of this sacred place, the god also known as Nataraja, Lord of the Dance, and as I look at him in a ceiling fresco, the spectacle before me is one of visual perpetual motion, with arms and legs contorted in all directions, yet with an unfathomable serenity on his face. With one leg he maintains complete balance while another flails, and his outstretched arms appear to be lifting up the world effortlessly. Shiva is the center of all activity, the culmination of endeavor. In the words of religion scholar R. C. Zaehner, "he dances in the sheer joy of overflowing power—he dances creation into existence."[21] Shiva reconciles all opposites: male and female, creation and destruction, human and divine. Dance can do that—so can God.

I note the irony of a Hindu shrine evoking so much internal movement, where the Hindus have been one of the earth's most stationary peoples, while the stones of the Kotel are so enormous as to be all but unmovable, and they are venerated by a people that has never been able to stay put.

Yet Hindus are the ones with Dancing Shiva. Jews are more often found sitting *shiva*.

Aside from the play on words (in Hebrew, *shiva* is seven, and sitting *Shiva* refers to the seven-day period of intense grief following a death), I imagine what it must be like to have been brought up in a world where hundreds of generations of one's forbears have worshipped in the same way at the same place. And despite foreign conquests, natural disasters and the invasion of modernity, the dance goes on.

The view of this Hindu temple is not live, nor does it depict dawn. The sky is white, cloudy white. The colors of the building are dark brown and muted; I see none of the spectacular clarity of Jerusalem. While my computer does not convey smell (a kink yet to be worked out), I imagine a certain mustiness. Some of the frescoes are fading, but they still manage to convey a life force that entreats the viewer to dance, and the eye to keep looking higher and higher. One imagines the Tower of Babel to have looked like this. Have they ever heard of Babel here? Do they understand the constraints, the weightiness of God's word? No, here God is a playmate, a dance instructor. God as Barishnikov. God flies.

A few years ago, I brought my then three-year-old Daniel to my synagogue's morning service. Midway through, he abruptly left our row and began running circles in the aisle, singing out letters of the Hebrew alphabet. Embarrassed, I coaxed him back to his seat. Later he told my wife Mara, "Daddy didn't want me to dance at temple today." It made me reflect on how so many religious institutions drain our kids of the passion, the pulp of prayer, and how only the lucky few survive to reclaim it when they are older. Okay, so the Dancing Shiva is a graven image. Minor technicality. Dancing wasn't patented by the Hindus; not even Zorba has a monopoly on it. Although Jews are historically long on verbosity and short on choreography, we have had our great Lords of the Dance as well, including Miriam, David and a host of Hasidic masters. A neo-Hasidic revival now is cutting across denominational boundaries because the joyous dance of the Baal Shem Tov is just what the hassled masses are looking for.

I dance, too. Just as my world is beginning to spin out of control, I am stabilized by the realization that, for me, as with Shiva, my movement is circular, and the spokes of my week radiate from a fixed center: the Sabbath. The Alexandrer Rebbe, quoting Isaiah, said, "'For you shall go out with joy.' This means: If we are habitually joyful, we shall be released from every tribulation."

So it's not the dancing that we do on the dance floor that matters. It's the dancing we do in our hearts.

I imagine the Kotel, the Meccan mosque and this Hindu temple, side by side by side, like the Protestant, Catholic and Jewish houses of worship built next to one another in the early days of the American suburban baby-boom era. Could these pilgrimage sites exist on the same street the way those homogenized Americans' edifices did? Can they exist in the same world? Can God hop from one to the other, constantly switching clothes and demeanors, from action to fervor to dance, from *Mitzvah* to *Jihad* to *Nataraja*? Can God be all three? Can I? I long to feel that joy, to generate that intensity of faith, and to make a difference in the world.

I am being called to criss-cross the globe. My picture is taking shape, but some major pieces are missing. If I were to visit a great European cathedral, a Chartres, or Notre Dame, or if I were to enter the Vatican, would I find there yet another side of God—and another way to approach God?

I must go there.

9

The God of the Fathers

Turn us into You, O Lord, and we shall return. Renew our days as of old.

—Lam. 5:21

You Can't Go Home Again.

—title of Thomas Wolfe's last autobiographical novel, published in 1940, two years before his death

A few nights after going online for the first time, I decided to run an immortality check. In the 1979 Steve Martin comedy, *The Jerk,* the main character is overjoyed to see his name in a telephone book, a watershed event signaling the end of anonymity. Unlike the protagonist of that film, I've had the privilege of seeing my name published in a number of places. But I needed to check out my immortality in cyber-space; so I clicked up one of the standard search engines and entered my name. "Joshua Hammerman" came up about a half dozen times, and I checked them all out. There were reprints of articles I'd written, and some chats about them, especially about a controversial piece I'd written for the *New York Times Magazine* a year earlier regarding circumcision. There were dozens of other Hammerman listings, involving Hammermans of all stripes: A think tank run by a computer wizard named Bill Hammerman, whom I had never heard of; a home page for a philanthropic organization run by a Stephen L. Hammerman, whom I wished I was related to. I even found a home page for my cousin Jan Hammerman.

And then I did a double-take. *I saw my father's name.*

My father, Michal Hammerman, had died suddenly of a

heart attack on New Year's Day, 1979, at the age of sixty. He had been beloved by his Brookline, Massachusetts, congregation as its cantor for thirty years. Suddenly, a decade and a half after he was taken from me when I needed him most (I was twenty-one and really struggling), there he was, before my eyes, alive in cyberspace. I clicked the mouse and, like a modern-day Dorothy clicking her heels, I discovered that one could go home again, not to Kansas, and not even to Brookline, but to *http://www.angelfire.com/biz/LikeJACKnMARIONS/ index.html.*

This site, a walking tour of mid–twentieth-century Brookline, is named for a restaurant that closed long ago: Jack and Marion's. This popular deli was where the locals hung out, and for all expatriates like me, its mere mention is enough to flood the mind with nostalgic recollections of the animated street life along the main drag in my part of town, Harvard Street. At the heart of Harvard Street stands my synagogue, Kehillath Israel, affectionately called K.I. by us locals. I roll past the introduction, noting that I do not recognize the name of the Webmeister, Michael Ross, then, just scrolling down just a bit more, my screen is filled with a photo of the imposing front facade of that very same K.I., my home, my father's home, the place where I came from.

Then:

> The Harvard Street environs of the late 1950s through the 1970s is fondly remembered by some for the following:
>
> —Irving's Candy Store with Irving and Ethel *[Irving's was the place just across from K.I. where I got*

all my baseball cards, Superman comics and those precious pre-Hebrew school Ring Dings.]

—Mr. and Mrs. Feldman's bakery *[Whose fresh-baked seeded ryes still melt in my mouth, and it's been years since the place closed.]*

—Mr. Hecht's drugstore *[Buddy Hecht, my dad's best friend, was a saint. The store was just down the street from K.I., so I used to go there during the two-hour break between public school and Hebrew school to have a snack or late lunch. Buddy made those old-fashioned Hamilton Beach soda-fountain milk shakes with the chocolate syrup running down the sides of the tall glass. My first exposure to traumatic change was in my early teens when Buddy closed his store. I cried. He went to work for C.V.S.]*

—Kehillath Israel's Hebrew School "Wise Men of Chelm" stories. with Messrs. Spack, Gomborow, Brun and Shindler. *[No need to burden you with those silly stories about simpletons of Jewish lore; suffice it to say that they are the mythical inhabitants of a real place, who were known for utilizing logic to its most absurd extremes. The teachers mentioned were the heart of the Hebrew school faculty, and for many they were the incarnation of the Wise Men of Chelm. But I happened to love Hebrew school. I was just weird, I guess.]*

—K. I.'s High Holiday tent (for teen services, which were packed by hundreds] *(The High Holidays in*

Brookline rivaled anything I've ever read about classic Jewish communities past and present, from Jerusalem to Flatbush to Vilna to Minsk. On Yom Kippur Eve, Harvard Street would be packed with people, all headed to one place, to hear one glorious voice—my dad's.]

—The *old* Coolidge Corner theater, most often featuring Rock Hudson, Doris Day and (yes) John Wayne *[I saw* Pinocchio *there three times.]*

—Playing baseball at Russell Playground *[Around the block from my house; I played lots more than baseball there. Every sport imaginable; especially street hockey, which was very popular during the Bobby Orr era in which I came of age.]*

—Babcock Street before the *new* fire station

—The *very* expensive S. S. Pierce store

—Pick a Chick's bagels *(I liked Eagerman's better, but the best were the chewy ones from New York that my father brought back from business trips.)*

—Rabbi Saltzman's fiery sermons *[He was the rabbi of K.I., one of the great orators of his generation, and an inspiration to over thirty graduates of the Hebrew school who themselves went on to become rabbis.]*

—Cantor Hammerman's warm, smiling, powerful voice [My God!]

It was my first week of being online, and *I found my father there!* The world of my childhood was reborn before my eyes.

When I first saw my father's memory invoked so lovingly, by a person I likely never had met whose name I did not recognize, distant memories came rushing back and feelings long dormant were revived. I was there again, eleven and playing dodge ball in the dusty outer courtyard of the synagogue, fifteen minutes before that dreaded bell would usher us into class. I felt myself ripping open a pack of baseball cards from Irving's, tossing the gum and scrutinizing the bunch for a Carl Yastrzemski or Jim Lonborg. And I could see my dad, the public Dad that everyone knew, who smiled and winked at me from the pulpit, and the even-warmer private one whom only I knew, running his fingers through my hair and calling me "sweetie."

I looked at the computer. This machine, this bunch of screws and wires and buttons, had provided me with an instant out-of-box encounter with my immediate ancestry; it had connected me to a part of my being that I thought no longer was there. It had transported me not sideways, but back, way back, to a world that had long since died for me, and to a father I still grieve for.

The experience was virtual, but the journey was real.

It was a turning unto God; and my days were renewed as of old.

When God is revealed to Moses at the Burning Bush, God says (Exod. 3:6), "I am the God of your father, the God of Abraham, the God of Isaac and the God of Jacob." Later commentators note that God had to be introduced in this way, rather than as the "God of Abraham, Isaac and Jacob," because each generation, indeed each individual, experiences God differently. Yet, as differing as our experiences of the sacred are, they are also cumulative. We do not create theological metaphors in a vacuum. While my soul doesn't resonate to the God-as-Shepherd metaphor, it does respond to the memory of my father, whose generation *was* moved by that image, leading a packed congregation in prayer. The God of my father lives through those memories of mine, intimate memories stirred afresh by the recollections of a total stranger.

10

The First Journey
Sacred Stones in Gentle Light

Envisioning Cathedrals in Chartres

I have surely built a habitation for You, the foundation for Your dwelling forever.

—1 Kings 8:13 (Solomon, dedicating the first Temple)

I try, on a whim, *www.vatican.com*. Don't bother. It's a crank, a tasteless doctored photo of the pope with exposed female legs and a Christmas tree on his head. It is tacky, but I can't help but wonder if this on some level is meant to interact with the three-breasted founder of Madurai, and how all of this is beginning to piece together like a Picasso painting. (To get to the real Vatican, by the way, go to *www.vatican.va*.)

I run an AltaVista search on Chartres, and the second link takes me not to the cathedral, but back where I began—to Jerusalem. I keep being pulled back to Jerusalem—and to the dawn. It's a firsthand account of the Crusader conquest of Jerusalem in 1099, written by a certain Fulk (or Fulcher) of Chartres, *(www.fordham.edu/halsall/source/fulk2.html)*:

> *And on the day following the seventh, in the early morning, the leaders ordered the attack, and, with the trumpets sounding, a splendid assault was made on the city from all sides. . . . Some Saracens, Arabs, and Ethiopians took refuge in the tower of David, others fled to the temples of the Lord and of Solomon. A great fight took place in the court and porch of the temples, where they were unable to escape from our*

gladiators. Many fled to the roof of the temple of Solomon, and were shot with arrows, so that they fell to the ground dead. In this temple almost ten thousand were killed. Indeed, if you had been there you would have seen our feet colored to our ankles with the blood of the slain. But what more shall I relate? None of them were left alive; neither women nor children were spared.

This was not the Chartres I was looking for, but perhaps a signal that I needed to see that so much of what I had been visiting was creating for me an aura of illusory placidity. The same early morning that could appear so peaceful on the Kotel Kam or in the vista of Mecca can also be a time for wading in pools of blood. That this eyewitness was describing such carnage, taking place in the exact same location upon which the Kotel Kam is trained, and at the exact same time of day, only reinforces that stark contrast and that symmetry. Fulk of Chartres was not only describing an important event in world history, but an indicator of the turbulent, but ultimately balanced inner life of God.

The next site brings me right where I want to be. The Earthlore Gothic Cathedral Profile of Chartres (www.elore.com/elore04c.html) has (at least on this visit) as its introductory quote another reminder of the vicissitudes of morning light. This, from Henry Adams: "For a first visit to Chartres, choose a pleasant morning when the lights are soft, for one wants to be welcome and the cathedral has moods, at times severe."

The site goes on to explain the Gothic obsession with light: "Necessity of light was the motive of the Gothic architects. They needed light and always more light, until they sacrificed safety and common sense to get it."

Through this site, I take a crash course in Gothic architecture. I come across this quote from a dedicated medieval quarry worker:

"We who cut mere stones must always be envisioning cathedrals."

Chartres, Notre Dame, the enormous stones of the Kotel, the intricate friezes of Meenanshi, the exquisite calligraphy on the mosaic exterior of the Dome of the Rock: all creations of the callused hands of the faithful. Weathered, tired, hewn though they were, these were people who were building God's place on earth, and they gained such enormous inspiration and strength simply by gazing heavenward, Samson-like. With the morning's light to guide me, I am learning how to construct cathedrals.

What shines through the art and architecture of Chartres is, most of all, a purity of faith. The symbol of that is Mary. To appreciate Chartres is to feel her presence in every stone, as the architects did, in every chiseled face, in every upraised eye.

II

The Web and the Weaver

As cloth in the hands of the weaver
    Who shapes its lines and folds
    Or leaves it unadorned to hang unseemly;
    So are we in Your hand, righteous God.

—Yom Kippur liturgy

*T*he prevailing metaphor of this new cybervillage we are creating, *the Web,* is how I think we all are beginning to think of God. "The Lord is my Web" might not sound right just quite yet, but it is beginning to feel right for so many of us.

A survey of the Hebrew Bible would not lead us to believe that "web" could possibly become a front-running candidate for divine imagery. In the Hebrew Bible, the term appears fewer than half a dozen times and typically has negative connotations. In the book of Job, one of Job's fair-weather friends, Bildad, lectures Job in chapter 8, saying, "So are the paths of all who forget God . . . his hope shall be cut off, and his trust shall be a spider's web." In other words, either the trust will tear apart as easily as a web or it will become ensnarled and bogged down. Either way, not good. And the next verse implies that the houses of the wicked are themselves like webs. Isa. 59:5–6 compares the evil plans of those who seek to thwart the righteous to the webs that the spider spins to catch insects. Ps. 140 mentions the spider and snake as examples of poisonous creatures.

Later Jewish sources aren't much more sympathetic. One

of the more famous teachings of the Talmudic sage Rav Assi (late third century), based on Isa. 59, is that the evil inclination, though initially as fragile as a spiderweb, eventually gains the firmness of a cart rope (tractate Sukkah 52a). Rabbi Nahman ben Jacob, who lived at about the same time, was known for the misogynous saying, "When a woman is talking she is spinning (a web to capture her male)" (Megilla 14b). In the New Testament, incidentally, the web doesn't appear at all, either as a concept or a metaphor.

From this angle, at the root of the web's image problem lies the age-old fear of spiders. According to the *Encyclopedia Judaica*, the Land of Israel has hundreds of species of spiders and all have poisonous glands in their maxillaries. While the poison in most spiders is far too mild to affect humans, it doesn't exactly create an aura of endearment around a creature that is rather creepy to begin with.

But through history, the web has also taken on different meanings, less associated with its spidery source. Anthropologists now claim that human beings were food gatherers before we were hunters and that the first human tool was not an axe or spear, but a basket. Knotting, tying and weaving were revolutionary discoveries, steeped in mystery and magic. In some societies, binding hair or clothing gave one control over that person's soul. In the book of Judges, Samson dares Delilah to weave his hair into a web as a means of sapping his strength. In ancient Greek mythology, the Fates (called Moerae) were three goddesses who controlled human life. They included Clotho, who spun the web of life; Lachesis, who measured its length; and Atropos, who cut it. In modern literature, webs have come to be associated with intricate plot lines. Webs are also associated with tangled tales of deceit, as exemplified in Sir Walter Scott's famous ditty,

> *O, what a tangled web we weave,*
> *When first we practice to deceive.*

In the twentieth century, Picasso saw artistic inspiration in the web and Antoine de Saint-Exupery "a mesh into which relationships are tied." That is exactly what Tim Berners-Lee had in mind for the world's scientists when he created the term "World Wide Web" in 1989. He likely didn't consider this quote of Seattle, chief of the Dwarmish, Susquamish and allied Indian tribes, who wrote in an 1854 letter to President Franklin Pierce:

> *This we know: the earth does not belong to man; man belongs to the earth. This we know. All things are connected like the blood which united one family. All things are connected. Whatever befalls the earth befalls the sons of the earth. Man did not weave the web of life: he is merely a strand in it. Whatever he does to the web, he does to himself.*[22]

Chief Seattle's words have become gospel to environmentalists everywhere (I even saw it on the menu of the Rainforest Cafe), and the foundation of many earth-based theologies. The second Adam and Eve, the main characters of the second Creation account, would have had little trouble relating to Seattle's passion. Most recently, the popularity of this philosophy of interconnectedness has found expression in the Gaia theory of the earth as a living system and various other systems theories in biology and physics that have moved us from an essentially mechanistic world-view to one that is more holistic. Spiritual-scientific synthe-ses have cropped up, such as those of Fritjof Capra, author of *The Tao of Physics,* and most recently *The Web of Life,* in which he writes,

> To regain our full humanity, we have to regain our connectedness with the entire web of life. This recon-necting, religio *in Latin, is the very essence of the spiritual grounding of deep ecology.*[23]

A second look at the ancient Jewish sages reveals that they, too, understood the power of the web metaphor in grasping the interrelatedness of all creation. The Babylonian Talmud is divided into sixty-three volumes, known as trac-tates, which were compiled and edited over the course of hundreds of years, until the collected work reached its final form around the year 500. In Hebrew, the word for tractate is *Masechet.* It so happens that the word also means "web." The labyrinth of collected academic discussions that make up Talmudic literature can best be described in that manner. One does not pick up a tractate of Talmud to gain quick answers to complex questions—in fact, the opposite is true. The Talmud gives us complex responses to what we might have thought were easy questions. Each Talmudic discussion brings us in to the inner world of its participants, often including rabbis of several different generations. Each argument is based on a logic process consistent with the thought processes and assumptions of that particular rabbi.

Like a good novel, the Talmud weaves a web of seemingly disconnected information, and by the end, somehow the strands come together to form a cohesive and meaningful whole. This finished web leads us to the conclusion that life is infinitely complex, that certainty is elusive, and that the process of searching for answers is more significant than actually finding them. More often than not, the Talmud doesn't give us the answers. The vast majority of the discussions found in its tractates remain unresolved.[24]

The word *masechet* is also found in a rabbinic commentary to the Psalms, known as *Midrash Tehillim,* and this quote, coming from around the time of the Talmud, helps us understand fully why that particular word was chosen to describe the interconnected and sacred nature of all areas of life; it also brings us to a most significant milepost on our journey: *"We are the web,"* it states, *"and You are the Weaver."*

We have left the shepherd behind us, as you recall, somewhere out to pasture. Now we are introduced to God the weaver, a new and engaging metaphor that turns out to be almost as old as that shepherd one. "The Lord is our Weaver" is an astonishing image, but it gets us only halfway home. The other half will be to see God, as well as all reality, as existing within the web itself, and then transferring that notion to the Web—the Internet—itself.

The fact that the word *masechet* is derived from "web" does not point to a cultural phenomenon that is uniquely Jewish. There is almost certainly a connection between *masechet* and the Latin word *textus,* which comes from *texere,* meaning "to weave, to fabricate." All texts consist of woven strands of ideas coming together to form a whole. Fittingly, they are printed on material that is itself woven, or they appear on electronic screens that consist of interconnected lines or dots.

Look around in our society today and see the popularity of web-like images in our language, including tapestries, patchwork quilts, knots, mosaics and labyrinths. When we see these metaphors in constant use, we must ask what the users are looking for. Most often the use of such imagery exposes a passion for interconnection and a desire for the security and order in a world that appears from close up to be such a mishmash. When former New York mayor David Dinkins called the city a "fabulous mosaic," he was looking at a city that, from close up, appeared to consist of segregated enclaves of various ethnic hues, but from a distance might be seen as an ensemble of complementary pieces. His assumption was that there was some manner of glue holding this mosaic all together. He might have considered himself that substance, though in Crown Heights the mosaic became unglued rather dramatically (just as it has more recently under Mayor Giuliani with the Diallo case and other accusations of police brutality). But on a different level, others might consider that glue to be God. A New York seemingly at peace with itself, with a lower crime rate and increased tourism, only enhances the power of the "fabulous mosaic" myth.

I remember as a teen holding on old LP of Carole King's *Tapestry* in my hand and how the record cover itself felt as if it were woven of wool or flax, and how good that felt to the touch. The songs only added to the sensation. For Jews, the act of holding the braided fringes of the prayer shawl (*tallit*) in our hands, as we are required to do for various prayers, but many do throughout the service, is a very comforting tactile experience. For me, it is the adult equivalent of holding my blankie, and indeed for many Jews, a lasting childhood memory is that of sitting in synagogue, fiddling with the fringes of a parent's *tallit*. Running between my fingers four sets of eight interwoven strings, knotted and wound together, I am asked by the tradition to be reminded of the cohesive nature of the divine commandments and of the unity of the Jewish people living in the "four corners" of the world. And doing this while other congregants are doing the same thing (men and women in my congregation) is an additional solidifying factor, along with the fact that the *tallit*'s traditional blue thread reflects the underlying unity of heaven and earth.

No doubt about it: We crave webbing. One might call this the "Fruit of the Loom" generation. While our forbears craved independence above all, for us, our most heartfelt prayers are declarations of interdependence. That 1980s' hit song "We Are the World" might have been unbelievably corny, but what other hymn could unite the diverse vocal talents of an entire generation? When I run the smooth tassels of my *tallit* through my fingers, at times I really do feel that "we are the world," that all reality is a neatly woven melange.

There might be only one other tactile experience that provides the same comfort for my fingers and blankie-like security for the rest of me, and that is when I put on my old webbed baseball mitt. In fact, my first night on the World Wide Web in the summer of 1995, described in the introduction to this book, will always be intertwined for me with another summer evening that took place only a few days before, while on vacation on Cape Cod with my family. The experiences are linked because each brought together father and son in an act of initiation, a sudden passage into a new world melding together the old and the new.

Ethan was four and it was his first baseball game, a Cape Cod League clash between the Yarmouth-Dennis Red Sox and the Orleans Cardinals. The two of us sat on the grassy hill above the first-base line, proud dad and excited son, each of us wearing our gloves and hoping to snag a foul ball. The boy's glove was spanking new, and Dad's was rather worn in comparison, held together by a string, in fact, where there once was solid webbing . . . oh, about twenty-five years ago. And on Dad's tattered glove was inscribed in fading magic marker Dad's name and childhood home address, written in the handwriting of Dad's dad, the one who had applied the saving string to my disintegrating webbing. We had a toss between innings, and the feel of that ball hitting the pocket of my glove, as if drawn to it magnetically, and nestling just perfectly between my thumb and forefinger, spoke to my soul of just what it means to "fit." Everything was in its proper place: the glove, the webbing, the ball; the moon, the base paths, Ethan and I. There was a profound sense of order to it all, and with that a sublime comfort. God was there.

And the questions poured forth. Why, if the pitcher is always throwing a ball, is it sometimes not called a ball? Why are there no girls playing? Why are the Red Sox losing?

I was able to field the questions deftly, even with my patched-up glove, and the evening turned to be one of those classic Norman Rockwell father-son things that could only result in lots of hugs, a misty eye or two and, by the end of the evening, another die-hard Boston Red Sox fan in the making. Through his dad's worn glove, Ethan could begin to see what doesn't change through the generations: three strikes and you're out, the timeless sensation of a cool summer night at the game—and that in the end the Red Sox always lose.[25]

When we sat in front of the computer screen a few days later addressing Whalermouth in an AOL chat room, again he was filled with questions, but this time I had no easy answers.

"How does this thing work?"

I have no idea.

"Is Whalermouth a real person?"

I suspect so.

"Is his name really Whalermouth?"

I suspect not.

"Why doesn't he use his real name? And why did you, Daddy, call yourself Hamrab?"

Because it's short for Rabbi Hammerman and yet it has ham in it, so it's a play on words. I'm trying to be funny. *Get it?*

I know that, just as he will someday hit a baseball much farther than his old man, soon Ethan will become far more adept than I in exploring this new complex technology. But will this new Web provide for him the comfort that my glove's old webbing gave me on that grassy hill and so many times before? Will he one day long to tell his children about the father-son experiences he once had in front of a computer screen? Will our relationship some day be made holier because, when inevitably he is living in Timbuktu and I just as inevitably in Florida, we will be communicating primarily through it?

If we are to speak of the Web as holy ground, then the experience of going online has somehow got to be as comforting as running that *tallit* through my fingers. It has to be more soothing than a blankie, because we can't just come out of the encounter feeling safe and secure—we've got to feel profoundly connected. And our souls must be touched primarily without the benefit of our physically touching anything. There is very little that is sensual about the tactile experience of flipping on a computer, clicking a mouse and tapping a keyboard. But in the end, that experience must feel as comfortable as that old baseball glove if it is to lift us to a higher reality.

12

The First Journey
Sacred Stones in Gentle Light

Kosovo and the Eternal Thread

As stone in the hand of the mason,
To be broken or preserved as he wishes,
Are we in Your hand,
Master of life and death.

—Yom Kippur liturgy

$\mathcal{M}$y pilgrimage is not nearly over. AltaVista presents me with a most perplexing stop on the itinerary: Kosovo. Renowned most recently more for torture and strife than peaceful inspiration, I click and enter this Balkan site with the curiosity of the modern-day Alice in Wonderland I feel I am beginning to become.

"A Pilgrimage to Kosovo Today" *(www.decani.yunet.com/ pilgrimg.html)* chronicles the 1996 journey of Ryanassaphore Nun Natalia, an Orthodox nun from California. I happen to be reading her lengthy account on a day when rising tensions between factions within this province are headline news in the *New York Times*. "I had no idea of the profound effect that this land and those whom we meet would have on my soul," she commences, and certainly had no idea how much of an impact her words would have on mine. I'm not really sure how this account ended up on a Website, given her clear antipathy toward modern technological culture, as contrasted with the village and farm life she encountered in Serbia. "Nowhere did you see a fast-mart gas station, suburban mall or fast-food restaurant," she writes. Instead, it was common to see horse-drawn carriages carrying mounds of hay, with geese and pigs running in front.

"No supermarkets are to be found; meals are made with bread

from a family's own wheat, cheese from their own cow and vegetables from their own garden. Picturesque haystacks dot the verdant
fields, and the simple white-washed houses with red-tiled roofs only
enhance the beauty of the countryside."

She calls this Eden-like scene "the original plan of salvation,"
something we urbanized Americans have lost irrevocably. "No
wonder there is such emptiness in the heart of our people," she
adds, "the natural way of life given to us has been replaced with
'virtual reality,' TV dinners and concrete jungles. No wonder so few
Americans are still willing to die for their country, or even to
express a love for it."

A willingness to die for one's faith is not a mere abstraction in
Kosovo, but a trait that has been tested often over the centuries.
Natalia details a litany of martyrdom as she hops among the
region's monasteries; and as she describes the massacres of the
long-suffering Christian Kosovars, I sense a sacred envy of sorts on
her part, one to which I can't relate. She writes (prophetically), "The
political situation in Kosovo right now is on the brink of explosion.
But in the words of Bishop Nikolai Velimirovic, 'Assuredly, one who
sacrifices everything for one radiant ideal has always emerged vic-
torious.' They are like lambs for the slaughter, who are joyfully
preparing themselves to join the heavenly choir of the New Martyrs
of Serbia."

My mind is flooded with uncanny symmetry: Crusaders murdering
Moslems on the Temple Mount; Moslems killing Christians in Kosovo,
Serbians now returning the favor, all for the sake of God. The placid
interplay of shadows and light at the pre-dawn Kotel; and here, at a
monastery built in 1315, considered to be the most beautiful in the
Orthodox world, I read, "In the alternating light and shadows,
Gracanica appeared to be the apparition of unreal beauty, which
inspired these verses from Desanka Maximovic: 'O Gracanica, if you

were not made of stone you would be raised to the skies.'"

A famous song about the Western Wall speaks of some people having hearts of stone and some stones having human hearts. Natalia speaks of the purity of faith being demonstrated in a willingness to die for it, which, like *Jihad*, could easily be misinterpreted as a willingness to kill.

I am uncomfortable with this and wish to leave Kosovo, but I read on, to this invocation to the ascetic founder of the Devic Monastery, found at the end of the journal:

> *We beseech thee, holy Ionannikoios of Devic,*
> *Lift up thy right hand, shield us . . .*
> *In the midst of fire and famine, keep us,*
> *And raise us up, and teach us on the field of calamity*
> *To build a City from the stones*
> *With which they stone us!*

She concludes the account with reflections made while driving with her companions back through the plains of Kosovo. "Every glimmering day," says one, "is another day in the struggle of the two kingdoms." Natalia asks, "Which kingdom shall I choose? Shall I choose the earthly kingdom? Or shall I choose the heavenly? The new sons and daughters of Serbia are slowly coming to this place of martyrdom, seeking to attain the cutting edge in the place where the battle is fiercest and the crowns are eternal. The monastics laboring on the ancient battlefield of Kosovo have already made their choice: to die an earthly death for the sake of the Heavenly Kingdom."

And then she adds, "Caught in the spirit of the moment, the young people in the bus break into the chanting of the hymn, 'O Gentle Light.'"

I wish to scream from my chair to her bus—the message is not to die! Martyrdom is not the supreme value! The heavenly kingdom could exist on earth, if only we would see that the supreme sacrifice is not what God wants of us. Just as *Jihad* does not require war, so does absolute faith not require martyrdom. I want to build that city of stone, too, but not a city to protect me from those who cast that stone; rather, a city so beautiful as to encourage them to lay their weapons down. And one can build such a city, even here, even among the golden arches, even, and maybe especially, if it is virtual.

I grab a Bible from the shelf and look for Ps. 118.

> *I shall not die! But I shall live and relate the deeds of God. . . .*
> *Open for me the gates of righteousness and I will enter and thank God. . . .*
> *The stone despised by the builders has become the cornerstone.*
> *This is the doing of the Lord—it is wondrous in our sight.*

The gentle, white light of dawn is God's reflection dancing on the stones, bringing them to life. These stones in their most elemental form are the "doing of the Lord," God's building blocks, granted renewed life by man's craftsmanship and perseverance, compelling us to choose life. God is everywhere, but the divine emanation is reflected most vividly on the rejected and resurrected cornerstones of God's places of pilgrimage.

I've learned this from my first online journey, from the preternatural repetition and intertwining of these motifs of light and stone, of martyrdom and renewal, found in sites as distant from one another as the human mind can imagine, but linked intrinsically through cyberspace.

I could stop here, but there is much more to see. I'm tired, even though my feet have been inactive, but there are several more stops on the itinerary and each is necessary to complete the picture. I've resolved to scan them quickly. It's well past midnight.

To regain my bearings, I return home to Judaism, for another firsthand pilgrimage account, that of an American-born Hasid who visited the grave of the venerated Rabbi Nachman, a sage who lived and was buried in what is now the Ukrainian Republic in a village called Uman (*www.pinenet.com/~rooster/uman.html*). What strikes me is the similarity between this pilgrim's passion and that expressed by the Orthodox nun—and how far removed it is from my own, more balanced approach. Orthodoxy, like mysticism, knows many garbs. This detailed journal chronicles intimate reflections; I know that I could never attain such insights in face-to-face conversation with this man. I doubt that he would pour his soul out to a liberal rabbi.

I click quickly over to another firsthand account of a Moslem pilgrim on *hajj* to Mecca, then to a site of the Temple Mount Faithful, a group of right-wing Jews anticipating the speedy coming of the Messiah and the building of a third temple on the site of what is now the Dome of the Rock. I imagine an inverse Kotel Kam, with the Wall completely engulfed in shadows. It is a foreboding reminder that the calamities recorded by Fulk of Chartres may be a prelude to a future destruction far more terrible. I hop to a Bahài site, then to a New Age itinerary of sacred sites along the Amazon, then to another, advertising Buddhist pilgrimage tours, claiming: "We live in Nepal. . . . We know Nepal. . . ."

And America, you are no Nepal.

Finally, fully three and one half hours after I began this journey, it is time to come up for air. It's very late—or very early. All I know for certain is that I am very tired.

What have I learned thus far in the gentle light of dawn?

To struggle over whether authentic faith must imply a willingness to die, while at the same time affirming with certainty the supreme value of life.

To understand that stones can be for building, attacking or throwing away, all for the sake of God. But the noblest use of all is building—building our visions.

And I've learned how people can be like stones: hardened, devalued—or raised to the heavens, as we are carved exquisitely by a divine hand. But all in absolute equality. We are all the same.

I recall the verse from the Talmud (tractate Avot): "Who is wise? One who learns from all others." It doesn't say all other Jews. It doesn't say all other men. It says all others. The killing seems so foolish when we are able to learn from all others, to see their faith as they see it, and to understand that it also ours. But so few do. The stone and the light of dawn are an eternal thread linking not only these pilgrimage sites, but also all of us, and God. The inner life of God can be summed up in a progression of sunrises and sunsets, and in the erosion, construction and vision of our sacred spaces. People visit such places and notice first the light and shadows, the interplay of eternity and temporality, the rise and fall, which causes them to reflect in wonder at our own eternal desire to dream, to build and to rebuild.

I don't feel that I have come face-to-face with God on this first online journey, but I do feel that I have found something of a God's-eye view of us, the perspective from the top of the highest cathedral, a place where God could worship. And I've come to understand more than ever the potential of our advanced technology to enable us to construct a new Tower of Babel, this time the right way, without hubris, stone by stone, brick by brick, with visions of cathedrals dancing in our eyes.

13

The Intimacy of Detachment

Being alone has its special value,
But only when one is among others.

—Rabbi Yitzchak of Vorki

Why should I feel lonely? Is not our planet in the
Milky Way?

—Henry David Thoreau, Walden

This path
No one walks along
Evening of autumnal day.

—Basho, Zen haiku

I know one thing for certain: God was present for me on that grassy hill behind first base. The question that I must answer now is: Was God present for me when I began to venture forth online?

Yes.

Yes. God was present when Ethan, Daniel and I wrote our first happy birthday email note to my then twelve-year-old niece, Luz, in Israel.

God was present a year later, when a dozen first cousins began to renew family ties by creating an email cousins' club. We did it following the tragic deaths of my aunt and uncle. Before their deaths, we had begun to talk of having a family reunion in the near future. Nothing would have made Aunt Ruth and Uncle Bernie happier. After the funeral, only a few days later, Ruth's daughter Marilyn proposed speaking of something more elaborate: a cousins' club online. Within a couple of months, those of us with email capacity were all signed on, I compiled a mailing list, and the cousins'-club-without-walls was born.

The distance that separates us, spanning from Israel to California to Georgia to New England—it all dissolves to nothing as we shoot the cyberbreeze at the beginning of each month in our virtual living room. We all had heard the tales of how our parents congregated each Saturday afternoon with their first cousins, in the Brooklyn living room of their *Zeydeh* (grandfather), whose name was Joshua. The Net is now Zeydeh's living room, without the hugging and honey cake perhaps, but with intimacy of another sort: the *intimacy of detachment.*

It's as simple as this. Communication is multisensual. When we meet others we sample scents (like dogs, though not quite as obviously), and we encounter people through sight, sound and touch, and maybe much later in the relationship, taste. Words are only one aspect of this multimedia sensual bombardment, and with each of us self-conscious about every other aspect of our presentation, heartfelt intimacy is not easy to achieve. The words easily get lost in the shuffle. Even on the phone, where our ears get in the way of our hearts, what we say is not necessarily what we really feel.

That great philosopher Fred Rogers, he of the neighborhood, put into a child's ditty what every adult longs to hear, the idea that true companionship and authentic communication transcends appearances.

> *It's you I like*
> *It's not the things you wear.*
> *It's not the way you do your hair,*
> *But it's you I like,*
> *The way you are right now,*
> *The way deep down inside you—*
> *Not the things that hide you,*

Not your toys—
They're just beside you.
But it's you I like.

As with many other traditions, in Jewish weddings it is customary for the bride to wear a veil. I tell this to every bride who is about to be veiled by her husband-to-be: the veil is not a sign of subservience or even of modesty, but rather of transcendence. True love transcends appearances. The veil, which denies both bride and groom the chance to see clearly the expressions on their loved one's face, allows them to see more clearly the image of God deep within the other.

Although I've never actually been in a room with all my cousins at the same time, we feel closer together as a group than was ever possible before. Even if our families had never left Brooklyn a generation ago, I don't believe we could possibly have become as close as we are today. The list is now nearing twenty, minus one beloved cousin who died recently of AIDS, and who was able to speak openly and intimately of his pain with his family most comfortably through email. The cousins' club has become so intimate, even though there may be a few whom I would not recognize if I passed them on the street. Such is the intimacy of detachment.

Alone/Together

The intimacy of detachment has communal implications as well. In Judaism, as well as other traditions, God is experienced most fully in a community. For the purpose of a complete prayer service, the minimal number of adults (over age thirteen) required to consider this group an official "community" or *minyan,* as it is called, is ten. Without ten, special prayers of sanctification (known by the Hebrew words, *Kaddish* and *Kedusha,* which mean "sanctification") cannot be recited. The implication is that God is not really as present, or at least as perceptible, without that number. The specific figure of ten was not randomly selected, but derived from the account of the twelve spies who scouted out the Land of Israel while the people still resided in the Wilderness. Ten brought back a negative report. And those ten are referred to in the text as an *edah,* a "community."

Yet when Jews pray, especially in a more traditional setting, much of the praying hardly sounds communal. People are all over the place, mumbling the Hebrew words each at a different pace, some mumbling in English, others humming, others dozing, still others discussing last night's ball game. There are certainly times when all are "on the same page" (especially during those prayers of sanctification), but for the most part, there is a strange paradox at play: People appear to be *alone, together.*

It is very liberating at a service to be able to focus on a single word or letter, to let your mind wander, to run your fingers through your child's hair, occasionally to chat with your neighbor or spouse, and to meditate on the big questions of your life.

But it is very comforting to know that people are around—an entire community, in fact, and one that cares for me. I can wrap myself in my blankie/*tallit* to hide from them, but when I need them, especially when making dramatic declarations about the meaning of sanctity, restoring order to my life, I can count on my neighbors to be there.

In a broader religious context, a key to experiencing God is through the ability to be alone, to have complete privacy, while also being able to unmask yourself unconditionally before the community. We see this at key life events, such as weddings and funerals, where tears flow unabashedly, in public, even while the participants or mourners are in the midst of a most private moment. For Jews, this is seen also on the High Holy Days, when the community atones collectively for the most personal of transgressions, including sexual misconduct and gossip. At my synagogue, during the final hour of the Day of Atonement, as the sun is setting on a grueling twenty-five-hour fast, we open the ark and invite worshippers to approach the sacred Torah scrolls. An astonishing parade ensues, as one by one, or in pairs, the broken-hearted advance slowly to the pulpit for a few moments of personal prayer. By the dozens they come to bare their souls before God—knowing full well that hundreds of their friends and neighbors are watching them; knowing, yet unabashed. That is what it means to unmask yourself unconditionally before the community.

The interplay of solitude and community are crucial even to faiths that, unlike Judaism, see asceticism as an ideal. In many traditions, the hero must wander in solitude as a prerequisite to reentering the community to impart sacred knowledge. The pilgrimage of self-discovery begins alone, but without a social connection, it is meaningless. Eastern religion focuses especially on self-discovery as a means to attaining enlightenment. The Hindu ascetic, the *sanyasi,* is freed from social obligations to explore the inner realm of the spirit; detachment and renunciation of the world around him are prerequisites to this return to the Source.

But although this ideal is solitude, even here the community is also prominent. In India there are some twenty million *sanyasis,* many living in about five million ashrams. These people in ashrams, who have renounced all ties to the world, still maintain social connections to each other, for the purpose of study and to meet practical needs. According to Wayne Teasdale, a monk and writer,

> *Solitude and community are not opposed but internally related, since everyone and everything are grounded in unity. This is the mystery of advaita, or non-duality, non-separateness, or unity: it is the mystery of distinction within unity. True community is rooted in the mystery of advaita. The sanyassi chooses solitude to realize experientially the unity of everyone and everything, the truth that all is within him; the community is also within him, in the cave of his own heart.*[26]

If the ultimate goal is to be at one with all creation, then the small worship community is the nuclear unit from which that spirit of oneness gestates. All members of the faith community, whether at a megachurch in the suburbs, or a monastery in the middle of nowhere, ideally share one purpose that all hold to—caring for one another with one heart. On occasion, faith communities are actually able to achieve this in real life. I sense it in my sanctuary often enough to call myself extremely lucky. But there are tremendous obstacles to maintaining that alone/together balance:

- People have to be comfortable with the language of

prayer and forms of the ritual, or at least with the idea of being able to be on different pages. Most novices are not.

- People have to like one another, or at least not dislike anyone in the group. Have you ever seen that anywhere?
- They have to be comfortable unmasking themselves and letting their souls merge with one another in the experience of communal sanctity, otherwise God cannot be perceived in their midst. It's not easy to accomplish.

But when we are alone in front of a blipping screen, there is sanctity and there can be community. You are truly alone, yet simultaneously in the presence of millions, and easily in the presence of a *minyan* who are like-minded. In any chat room, by definition, if there are ten people in the room who choose to be there because of that basic concern, whether it be saving the whales or nominating Jerry Springer for president, these are ten like-minded people. The masks come off, the hearts merge, and the aloneness is transcended.[27] The experience of finding that *minyan* is incredibly powerful, obliterating boundaries, dissolving differences.[28]

Remember that Xerox commercial of the 1980s where the monk eschews the old painstaking method of copying sacred texts by hand for the more modern option of photocopying? Well, imagine if the great ascetics of the ages had had the chance to meet one another online. One could maintain a vow of silence while engaging in a myriad of conversations. One could steadfastly explore the depths of solitude and yet never be isolated. And if a desert sojourn was warranted to fulfill a solemn vow or a stage of pilgrimage, a sturdy, sand-resistant laptop would come in handy to nurture the community back home with insights of profound wisdom.

Would that solitude be compromised by our being so connected? Would the soul be unable to soar while enmeshed in this web? To think that is never to have been online late at night, in a dark corner of the house, all others asleep, no external noise. My computer room is hardly an ashram or monastery, but it is a sanctuary of sorts; a zone of security and purpose. I won't call it a place of order, because the strewn folders, CD-ROMs and books (primarily of the "For Dummies" genre) place that room pretty much in the "without form and chaotic" category of Gen. 1:2. Yes it is disorderly, but it is connected, as connected as any sanctuary in the wilderness or Temple in Jerusalem.

While most Jews worship collectively in synagogues, there is nothing that is less holy about a home. The ancient rabbis called the home a *mikdash me'at*, a microcosm of the temple. Ironically, the prayer Jews recite when entering their synagogues refers back to Num. 24, where the Moabite prophet Balaam, setting his gaze on the Wilderness (24:1), sees the family abodes of the people he intended to curse but instead blesses them, saying, *"How lovely are your tents, O Jacob, how fine your encampments, Israel."* The focal point of sanctity is the home, not the synagogue, temple or shrine, not the place of public cultic activity.

That same prayer includes several verses from Psalms, assembling them in a first-person singular form. *"As for me, drawn by Your love, I come into Your house. I lay me down in humble surrender, before Your holy shrine in awe . . . I greet, I bless, I bend the knee, before God who fashions me. And as for me, my prayer is for You;*

may it be a time of desire." Almost all Jewish prayer is recited in the first-person plural. But here, in the words of Rabbi Arthur Green, the prayers are "introduced in the halting and somewhat unsure voice of the individual, expressing some of that inadequacy that each of us feels as we enter the place and hour of prayer."[29] We don't have to be with others to pray. In fact, the Hebrew term for prayer is reflexive, and it literally means, "to inquire of oneself." To talk to God is to be in touch with our deepest selves, that which resides at our center. We can be alone to do that, and the holy place can be our own homes.

The great nineteenth-century Hasidic master Rabbi Nachman of Bratzlav wrote, "It is good to have a special room set aside for sacred study and prayer, secluded meditation and conversation with God."[30]

Sit down in front of your computer after midnight and see what is there. Reach out to connect—and not necessarily with people. Simply connecting to the latest news, to stock results or late ball scores, is enough to evoke a feeling of "humble surrender" and awe. How lovely can this universe be, how orderly and sound, when, without waking a soul, I can order cut-rate plane tickets to Chicago? How close to the mountaintop can you ascend, when, with a few clicks, you can see the deep blue earth from the perspective of a roving satellite hundreds of miles up? How dusty must my weary pilgrim's feet get, when I can click my way to a live shot of Jerusalem's Western Wall in seconds, and fax my prayer to be placed within its ancient cracks? Mircea Eliade, a modern master of the study of the Sacred, writes of a sacred space as a place of breakthrough, a point of passage to another realm, an absolute reality.[31] From where can we jump off into that higher world if not from a springboard whose range appears so limitless? Who would have thought that the "road less traveled" could be so easily located on the Information Superhighway?

If late at night, my Web-surfing brings me serendipitously to a challenging text or eye-opening story, the clicks and whirrs of the machine ebb and bequeath a soft silence; as I ponder what's on the screen for a few moments I can almost hear the whirring and clicking going on in my own mind. Sometimes I type in a random name or phrase, add a standard suffix (such as ".com"), and see what turns up. Once I checked out *www.joshua.com* and was whisked to "Joshua's Home Page." I met Joshua Wachs, a young Bostonian adult with lots of family pictures, a yen for volleyball and magic, and the smarts to be the first Joshua to apply for the *joshua.com* address. Sometimes I connect with my various rabbinic chat groups. Clergy are among the loneliest people I know, and, in many denominations, our chat groups have changed all that. We now have an outlet for sharing ideas, resolving problems and, most importantly, venting. Sometimes all of this feels like I am talking to God.

There are times when being online helps me feel completely centered, at peace and connected both to all that is Out There and deep within. That is what the early Hasidim called *hitbodedut,* a state of self-seclusion, where a person can have an unfettered conversation with God. Rabbi Nachman taught that we should seclude ourselves with God each day for at least an hour,

and speak with Him about everything that is going on in your life. Confess to Him all your sins, transgressions and failings, and speak to Him freely as one speaks to a friend. You should speak at length, talk and talk some more, argue with Him, sigh and weep, and ask that He have mercy and allow us to achieve true devotion.[32]

The act of introspective emailing/prayer, whether it takes the form of a correspondence with a loved one, a clergy, or a long letter to ourselves, allows us to be alone/together with ourselves and God. Sometimes, especially just before the High Holidays, I will reread some of my emails from the past few years. These letters to others are really letters to myself, as they enable me to explore the paths I have chosen, evaluate where I've veered from the original course and decide what corrections need to be made. This self-examination is a manner of talking to God.

For many of us, life in cyberspace has evolved its own rituals. We can't spend our entire lives there—we need to return to earth at some point. In fact, I have little time to devote to this sanctuary, so I go through a similar routine on most nights: I answer personal email and correspond to my various congregational and family lists, check out the next day's news from Israel and the sports from Boston, explore my temple's Website and various Jewish and other spiritual options, and then move on to other things. Occasionally, I'll just search for something obscure: a person from my distant past, a place I plan to visit, or a concept I'm planning to develop into an article or sermon. On occasions, I'll run another Hammerman immortality check.

No matter how ridiculous or sublime, no matter how disjointed all these bits of information appear, they all come from the same Place, and all are handed directly to me. Thus, they are connected, and all Reality is interconnected. Including me.

Breaking Down Barriers

We find God on the Internet because it binds us all as One.

The *Sh'ma,* that central affirmation of monotheism from Deuteronomy, is speaking not about an abstract being "out there," but as that glue, that woven knot, that web, that binds us all. Jewish theologian Arthur Green has written,

> In it we declare that God is One—which is to say that humanity is one, that life is one, that joys and sufferings are one—for God is the force that binds them all together. There is nothing obvious about this truth, for life as we know it seems infinitely fragmented. Human beings seem isolated from one another, divided by all the fears and hatreds that make up human history. Even within a single life, one moment feels cut off from the next. To assert that all is one in God is our supreme act of faith.

Think about it:

When we receive email, unless the corespondent specifies where he or she lives, the geographic address remains unknown—and irrelevant. The artificial barriers of space are broken down.

When I read the Israeli newspapers every evening before I retire, I'm reviewing the stories that my Israeli sister is just waking up to. Even though we live seven time zones apart, my spiritual clock is in Jerusalem. The barriers of time have been obliterated.

When Ethan checks out the major league baseball scores on the ESPN Website, then shifts to my synagogue's site to see himself and his brother Daniel listed along with other kids on our temple's junior baseball league (our teams are the Thunder and Matzah Balls), his uniqueness as an athlete and a human being are placed on the very same level as that of Sammy Sosa and Pedro Martinez. This dissolves artificial barriers of talent, income and age, affirming that all human beings are of equal and infinite worth.

When, with just a few clicks, I can gain access to resources of rabbinic commentary larger than the combined libraries of all the great rabbis throughout the ages, the barriers of access to knowledge have been washed away.

When a single click can shuttle me from Gingrich to Greenpeace, from Alvin Toffler's conservative "third-wave information age" to what Frank Rich has called a "whopping stealth victory for the counterculture," we have dismantled the intellectual boundaries separating left from right. The Internet is a grand party to which everyone is invited, and which everyone has in common. Everyone is part of the same single in-group. Everyone, that is, who has access to it—and as computers become more common in public schools and the Internet more affordable and available through other means (e.g., cable television), that access will become increasingly democratized. The Internet is the first real Main Street that we've ever had.

Let's face it, even those romanticized old bowling leagues and other social and service organizations have hardly been places where masks routinely come off. Sure, people socialize, but how often did Ralph Kramden release his inner child in front of Ed Norton at the Lodge? Online, this happens, constantly. And Main Street, that mythic place where everybody knows your name, does that really exist in the non-cyberworld? Did it ever?

For the past several summers, I've rented a home in the same small town on Cape Cod. Unlike much of the Cape, this town still has a real Americana feel to it: elderly gentlemen talking politics on the porch of the General Store, white picket fences, quiet beaches. I love these escapes; for me it is like going home again—to a place that never really was home.

One Sunday morning a few years ago I had a rather disturbing revelation. I was wheeling the stroller back from the General Store, having picked up my Sunday *New York Times* and *Boston Globe.* I passed all these other people carrying their *Hartford Courants, Worcester Telegrams* and *Providence Journals,* and of course to each his or her own *New York Times,* and all of us were saying "hi" to one another. People who were jogging stopped in their tracks to greet me. People on bicycles slowed down to exchange pleasantries. "What a friendly town this is," I thought. "Pity none of these people actually lives here." Indeed, few of us would be so friendly if we were on our home turf.

Then as I walked to my rented house I noticed that almost every car on the street had an out-of-state license. It was as if all the natives had left town and some aliens from outer space had taken over their homes, their stores, their driveways and their lives. We were pretending to be natives. My friend, Tom actually does live in that town. That summer he took his family to Guatemala. Why? "Too depressing to stay home," he told me. "We go to the beach and don't know anyone."

We want that feeling of community so much that we are willing to pretend that we live in a place in order to achieve it, even to the point of pretending that people are neighbors when we have no idea who they are and know that they actually live a state or two away. So you tell me, which community is real and which is virtual?

The mythical Main Street, that enduring icon of American mythology, that gathering place for friends and neighbors bound together by common memory and common purpose, *never really existed*. That idyllic place where complex issues never arose, pedestrians were never assaulted, nobody was poor and rain never fell, was never more than a figure of our fantasy. Yet we yearn for that feeling of home, for a place where no one will prejudge us by the color of our skin, the beauty of our face, the flatness of our stomach or the foreignness of our accent. It cannot be found at the mall. It can hardly be duplicated at the ball game (where gloves come off more often than masks), and it is even elusive in our places of worship. But we've found it in front of that blipping screen. Because that screen, more than anything else ever discovered by humankind, allows human beings to be *alone/together*.

14

The Second Journey
Beyond Good and Evil:
Revealing the Hidden Things

Who Forms Light and Creates Darkness

The Holy One, praised be He said:
"Even though I have hidden My Face from them,
nevertheless, I make Myself known to them in a vision."

—Talmud (Chagiga 5b)

*N*ow that we've tested this process, we move on to something that gets to the core of our relationship with God: the question of good and evil. The modern theologian Richard Rubenstein has written,

> In the aftermath of the Holocaust, the religious problem of evil raises questions that go to the very heart of Israel's perennial understanding of its relation to God. . . . it may be that the metaphor for understanding . . . (that relationship) must give way to an as yet unformulated new metaphor.[33]

What is true for Israel is true for all modern people with a conscience. We can't complete our quest for new metaphors for God until we have grappled with the question of evil.

I enter this journey armed with two presuppositions. One is that God is responsible for both good and evil in the world. The second is that God might not be.

I base my first conclusion on Isa. 45:7, where God is declared to be the One who "forms light and creates darkness, who makes peace and creates evil." This view is reinforced in the book of Job, where God speaks, finally, to the stricken Job, out of a raging whirlwind, and lets Job—and all of us—know that God is both all-powerful and unknowable. Evil, like everything else, is part of God's domain, and we can't even come close to understanding why good people suffer.

I take my second conclusion from Deut. 31:17. There God informs Moses that when the people commit evil deeds, "I will hide My face from them (V'histerati panai mehem), they will become prey, and will encounter evil to the extreme." This answer points to a God who might well have created evil originally but who, by design, has imposed restrictions on His own ability to control it, and to control us. God has become hidden, taken a back seat, and the problem of evil has been thrown into our court.

Just a few verses before that one, Moses tells the people (Deut. 29:28), "The hidden things (hanistarot) are for the Lord our God, but the revealed matters (haniglot) are for us and our children forever, to enact all the words of this Torah." This is one of the most mysterious and potent verses of the entire Bible. On the surface, it seems to be teaching us not to worry about things beyond our control, that we shouldn't get all caught up in theological or mystical speculations. Let God worry about those, it is implying, while we just go about our lives acting with justice and kindness. It's not dissimilar to the message Job got. But it is curious that the exact same Hebrew root word for "hidden" (in slightly different forms) is used in two verses not very far apart. In one case, God is hidden because of evil, and in the other case God has hidden specific information from us. Using the traditional interpretive tool known as remez (deducing allusions from similar words in juxtaposed verses), we can join these two verses together and allude that what is hidden from us might have something to do with evil.

"But the revealed matters are for us and our children forever." In the Torah, something astounding is found in this verse. Eleven dots appear over the words "us and our children." We have no idea why. Some say early scribes put them in for emphasis. Undoubtedly they do call attention to the verse—but to emphasize what? There is something extremely important about this verse, something that someone somewhere knew would become evident to "our children," sometime far into the future.

Perhaps that future is now.

God is becoming less hidden with every cybermoment. The Talmudic quote I've used at the beginning of this chapter seems curiously prescient, as the ancient sage Rava suggested that the God who had been hidden would come to be revealed in visions. There is a visionary, prophetic nature to the way the Internet is transmitted and received—this is a notion that I'll develop further in a later chapter. And as more of God is being revealed, we are becoming more adept at fighting evil, a task that truly has been thrown into our court. God is helping us to help ourselves.

And how is God being revealed to us in this context?

Through the exposure of evil itself.

I'll return to this shortly, but first, some more background on this question of evil. When the ancient rabbis incorporated the verse from Isaiah (calling God the creator of "good and evil") into the daily liturgy, they performed a bit of surgery on it, changing "creates evil" to "creator of all." Now one might assume that "all" includes evil, so why would they alter the original? To protect God's image?

Maybe it was because one of these sages, at some point, lost a child to pneumonia, or witnessed the martyrdom of a colleague, and had to ask that unavoidable question, why? When Rabbi Harold Kushner wrote his now-classic book on this subject, *When Bad Things Happen to Good People,* he tended to support the idea that evil is just not in God's repertoire. After the Holocaust, the ultimate evil event, many have struggled greatly with that question. If God is behind evil as well as good, how could God allow such an extreme form of evil to be perpetrated? But if God was not behind that excessive form of evil, how could God still be God? Any post-Holocaust theology must take into account the idea of an all-powerful God allowing innocent children to be thrown into the flames. That is almost impossible to do unless we think of God having chosen to become hidden and leaving the battle against evil for us to fight. This is, incidentally, a popular kabbalistic notion, dating from the great Rabbi Issac Luria of the sixteenth century. This voluntary self-eclipse of God is known as as *tzimtzum,* and the process of repairing the world, thereby restoring God's fullness to our earthly realm, is called *tikkun.* This is a battle that God wants us to win, because God has a deep stake in that triumph. And now, with our desktop vision machines, we have been granted the greatest possible weapon in that eternal battle, one far more powerful than a nuclear device.

So, what will we find on this expedition? Are there clues embedded in the darkest parts of cyberspace that indicate that evil can lead us to where God is hidden, and help us to help God emerge from this self-imposed eclipse? Will the Net show us that evil is unbounded, or actually well-balanced by the good?

This search will by its very nature take me to places I'd never have dared to visit before, the darkest places I can find. I expect that I'll not be recording all the addresses of these places, as the last thing I'd want to do is give hate groups or depraved deviants more exposure. I also expect that when I come up from air after this journey, I'll have begun to know something of what it must have been like to be Job, face to face with the Whirlwind.

15

God Lives in a Word

And the writing was the writing of God, engraved
on the tablets.

—Exod. 32:16

$\mathcal{A}$ lone in front of a blipping screen, what matters most are the words.

In the beginning there was the Word, and the Word was with God, and the Word was God. He was in the beginning with God, all things were made through him, and without him was not anything made that was made. In him was life. (John 1:1)

John's personification of the Word as partner in Creation has its roots in both Jewish and Greek thought. Plato wrote of such a blueprint for the Creation process, and the Jewish philosopher Philo refined it in the century before the birth of Christianity. For Jews, the Torah is that blueprint; for Christians, the Word is Jesus himself. If one takes Islam into account, it is clear that Western religious tradition is centered on the sanctity of the written word. *The Oxford Annotated Bible* describes John's "Word" (*logos* in Greek) as "more than (God's) speech; it is God in action, creating, revealing, redeeming." According to Rabbi Abraham Joshua Heschel, "God lives in a word." But, he adds, "Words can only open the door, and we can only weep on the threshold of our incommunicable thirst after the incomprehensible."[34] Despite the growing focus on graphics, video and sound, the experience of God online begins with the Word, though it can't possibly end there.

We find God on the Internet through the redemptive power of the written word.

On the Internet, God lives not exactly in the "written" word, because the words we see on the screen aren't really written. Like God, they are real, but can't be touched; they stand clearly in front of us, yet are primarily a product of the imagination, as our eye fills in the spaces between the lines and creates the impression of permanence.

It is against Jewish law to erase the name of God. That is why the Hebrew name of God (the tetragrammaton, as it is called, which consists of the letters *yod-heh-vav-heh)* is rarely spelled out in Jewish texts and most often is seen in an abbreviated form. Some even shorten the English appellation, using G–D rather than God. Yet God's name is all over the Internet, in all forms. Why? Because as the name appears on the screen, it is not in fixed, permanent form. It can be compared to writing your name with your finger on a frosty window.

A leading Orthodox rabbi recently ruled that the word "God" may be erased from a computer screen or disk, because the pixels do not constitute real letters. Rabbi Moshe Shaul Klein published his ruling in an Israeli computer magazine aimed at Orthodox Jews, *Mahsheva Tova.* "The letters on a computer screen are an assemblage of pixels, dots of light, what have you," the rabbi's assistant, Yossef Hayad explained to a reporter for the Associated Press. "Even when you save it to disk, it's not like you're throwing anything more than a sequence of ones and zeroes. It's there, but it really isn't."[35]

So the name of God isn't really being erased, because it never was really there in the first place. Or was it?

The words are virtual, just as the online relationships are virtual. Just as our relationship with God appears virtual, cloaked in metaphor. But it all feels so real—because it is.

Through the word, we have come to a new understanding of reality. For the Internet is a medium of the word. True, there are graphics too, and now increasing capacity to communicate via audio and video images, but when the medium was developed in the late 1960s, its goal was to connect computers in their language so that academicians could communicate in ours—and ours happens to be words. The medium was intended originally as a depository of massive amounts of recorded data. When Tim Berners-Lee first proposed the World Wide Web near Geneva in 1989, his intent was to make scientific papers available on the Internet to other scientists. Graphic images were then added to words, but in the beginning, it was all about words. And that is still how we primarily know it.

So now we live in a world where billions of invisible words are out there, massive virtual libraries, information on almost everything imaginable. It's real yet untouchable, at our fingertips, yet without a computer it's impossible to fathom. Try explaining the Internet to those who have never experienced it—it's almost as impossible as explaining the Red Sea splitting to those who slept through it.

Think of how email has restored to us the power and romance of the written letter. True, there is nothing that can replace the feel of that letter from a loved one in your hand, the scent of the perfume, perhaps, and the anticipation of ripping the envelope and excitedly removing its contents. I agree that there is little romance in having a virtual voice exclaim, "You've got mail!" Nonetheless, ask yourself how many perfumed letters you've written lately, and why most people have eschewed that time-tested—and time-consuming—method. In spite of its imperfections, email has enabled us to rediscover what we once knew but forgot long ago, that our words can heal.

I knew that even before I began to fully implement the technology. A rabbi friend had told me of how several concerned members of his congregation had emailed him to "talk" about the terrible abduction and murder of an Israeli soldier. But they weren't really talking. They were writing. And email, in spite of all the bad grammar and annoying abbreviations, is still one step removed from the immediacy of a telephone or in-person conversation. Sometimes that extra moment can be enough to enable us to express ourselves as would a Cyrano de Bergerac.

The power of words can best be perceived when each word is surrounded by space, and when they are accompanied by silence. There is little silence when words are spoken; there is too much background noise, and too much pressure to volley a comment in return. On the radio, "dead air," as it is called, is lethal for ratings. On the telephone, it is lethal for conversation. When one party allows the line to go silent, it can only be for one of two reasons, and neither one is good: (1) too shaken to respond or (2) not listening. But with email, we know that what we say *here* is heard *there;* and the response is typically a response of the whole person—not just the mouth.

The *intimacy of detachment* lies behind the power of the confessional booth for Catholics. The confessor is able to strip off pretenses and bare the soul when there is direct contact filtered through a physical barrier allowing for anonymity and a modicum of distance, while also allowing for direct verbal communication and an instant response. But even in that booth the fact that communication is vocal can impede the raw intimacy of the words. Imagine such a situation where any self-consciousness about the person's own voice is also eliminated. The computer could become the confessional booth of the twenty-first century. In some ways, it has already become that for my congregants and myself.

Once I began to communicate with congregants by email a few years ago, I knew right away that I was on to something very important for our relationship. For years I had struggled with the question of how to reach out to hundreds of families to be an effective pastor for each of them. The key was to establish a degree of trust and intimacy, but for the vast majority, those who weren't intimately involved in educational projects, leadership programs, meetings or services, that intimacy would have to wait for life-cycle events to come. Typically, it is at the time of illness or death that a pastor and a family "bond." It's rather depressing to think that it will take over six hundred deaths for me to get to know my entire congregation. There had to be another way. There was.

My first email to the congregation list was sent out on November 25, 1996. It might not have been the shot heard round the world, but it had an instant impact. Here's a segment:

Dear Congregants,

You are part of history: the first email transmission on our Beth El congregants list. Right now the list is about twenty strong, consisting of those of you who have given me your addresses or emailed me over the past few months. The list will grow dramatically over the coming weeks as congregants hear about it in our mailings (and from you). The advantages of a "congregants list" are obvious: instant communications, enabling us to let you know about funerals for instance, important meetings and programs, schedule changes and to otherwise answer questions of general interest. In the not-too-distant future, I hope to be able to set up a "listserve" that will be more interactive so that you can talk to other congregants, but although this format is more one-sided (me talking to you), you are free to email me with your feedback, which I can forward to others on the list. Let me know if a matter you bring up is something you would want to share with other congregants.

Shalom from Cyberspace
Rabbi Joshua Hammerman

I created three congregational lists: one with basic news of meetings, deaths, births, etc., along with my assorted diatribes on subjects of common concern; a second focusing on Israel and current events; and a third with an emphasis on continuing education and textual study. I've since consolidated my effort. I now send out to the entire list, including a supplementary group of unaffiliated GenXers, a weekly dispatch containing a variety of information. I call it the Shabbat-O-Gram since it typically arrives on the eve of the Sabbath. This weekly ritual helps us to adjust our inner clocks to the rhythms of sacred time. We started with 20 or so on the list, and now, over three years later, we are at 160. It helped to have made some crucial announcements on the list during times of great internal controversy. Those who had been lagging suddenly subscribed to be in the know. Email, in fact, has redefined who is in and who is out in my congregation. Typically in religious institutions, the in-group, the ones who are really in the know, are the core, active members, who participate most in services and leadership activities and are most comfortable with the forms of worship. Every congregation has its core and peripheral groups, although the consistencies of these groups are constantly shifting. The greatest challenge for any pastor is to get the periphery to feel comfortable enough to come through that door. The great success of the megachurches is that they've been able to do that.

With email, another gateway has been created. Those people on the list, and those others who have access to our Website, are most definitely the congregants in-the-know now, whether or not they set foot in the building or otherwise see my face more than once or twice a year. There must be something magical about the words that I send out over cyberspace; because unlike any of my newsletters sent out by snail mail, the cyber mail is actually *read*—and faxed or forwarded to the darndest places. Maybe it's because of that sanctuary effect described above, where the ritualistic tapping into one's cyberworld has become such a sacred activity, a moment of connection, for people, that the first thing they look for is email from their rabbi. Suffice it to say that some of those who are not yet online, and that means primarily those of the older generation, have at times been extremely upset about this, although this problem has dissipated as Internet usage has become more widespread. A few remain in the out-group in two respects: uncomfortable with services *and* inaccessible by email. I may have to train them in Hebrew and Windows at the same time.

When a few hundred congregants, or about sixty college students on another list, read a letter I send by email, although it was "mass produced," it has the impact of a personal note from their rabbi, far more intimate than any form of mass communication I know of, including the sermon. Why? Is it because of the sacred aura of connection conveyed by this medium? Is it because many open their email in the intimacy of their pajamas? Or is it because with email it is so easy to respond?

With email, congregants discuss matters with me that simply don't come up even in the most private of telephone or office conversations. They feel freer to offer constructive criticism, or other suggestions about the temple; they ask obscure and not-so-obscure questions of Jewish law, things (e.g., why do we wave our arms and cover our eyes when lighting Sabbath candles?) that they might not have been ashamed to ask to my face, but just never would have gotten around to asking. But once they have an opened missive of mine on their screen, even on a subject unrelated to their question, all they have to do is click on "reply" and ask away. I hear about their troubled marriages and frustrating children, and also all the proud-parent stuff. I also hear from the children, of all ages, which is especially satisfying.

For college students, email from me is like a sweet reminder of home, especially when it comes during the crush of finals or the supreme anxiety of freshman orientation week. I never miss a chance to wish them well at holiday time, which can be especially lonely for someone missing a family Seder for the first time or celebrating Thanksgiving overseas. The ancient rabbis said that a simple visit to an ill person removes one-sixtieth of the sickness. In that case, my email to college students likely removes a similar amount of their homesickness, if not more.

The effectiveness of email in my ministry is admittedly anecdotal. I can't claim that Americans as a whole have become more receptive to the Word of God as delivered from their clergy because of it. I do know that hundreds of study groups have sprung up online, on Jewish texts alone. I do know that millions have become exposed to sacred study who otherwise would never set foot in a house of worship. Everything else is conjectural—including this:

There is a direct experiential correlation between traditional notions of revelation and prophecy and the way cybercommunications are received.

I'm not just speaking of 2:00 A.M. in a dark cubicle, but even at noon in the office. There is something about the experience of receiving the Word via Internet connection that parallels how the Word was received by our ancestors, in a manner unlike any previously known methods of communication. God talks to us better through this medium.

P.S. I'd be delighted to add you to my Shabbat-O-Gram email list. Simply email me at *rabbi@tbe.org*.

16

The Second Journey
Beyond Good and Evil:
Revealing the Hidden Things

Trumping the Racists

*G*od *is dead.*

—Nietzsche

*N*ietzsche *is dead.*

—God

—noticed in a bathroom stall on the third floor
of the Rockefeller Library, Brown University, c. 1977

*I*t's about 10:00 P.M. again, a time I'm finding to be optimal for these journeys to begin. The kids are asleep, my other work is put aside for the moment, and Internet access is relatively unfettered. I do a couple of searches on good and evil, but this journey is going to be run a little differently. With a few exceptions, I'm going to follow a word-association pattern. If an idea or expression comes to mind, say "evil" or "sin," I'm just going to slap a ".com" or ".org" on it and see what turns up.

My first try is *www.goodvsevil.org*, and, bingo, something comes up: an experiment in human nature coordinated by a foundation called the Athens Institute. They run positive and negative news links side-by-side, and ask the public to vote on which ones they prefer. We can choose to hop to the Positive Press, featuring stories about human triumph, perseverance and kindness. Or, if our blood pressure is too low, the Daily Outrage will get it pumping with features about "larcenous lawyers, hypocritical politicians and injustice from Alaska to Africa."

I go to the Positive Press first and am comforted by the positive quote of the day, from Eleanor Roosevelt: "The future is for those who believe in the beauty of their dreams." I take a look at the archives and see another quote that I especially like, from Mary

Pickford: ". . . for this thing we call failure is not the falling down but the staying down." Great sermon material here, I note.

I go next to The Daily Outrage and find myself in extremely familiar territory. This is tabloid country, filled with juicy anecdotes about everyone in Washington, Hollywood and anyone else who has ever spent a night in a bedroom without actually sleeping. Their quote-of-the-day, taken from Thoreau's *Civil Disobedience*, advocates the right to revolution in the face of a tyrannical government—hardly something I would put in the evil category. But that brings up an important point in defining terms. Evil is synonymous with chaos, not necessarily with "badness." Revolutions are chaotic, not always bad. Government scandals are chaotic, too, even when the depravity hasn't been proven. This reinforces my presumption that the opposite of evil is not necessarily good, but God. Evil exists where there is an absence of God, since God is the "embodiment" of order. Evil exists where God is hidden, where there is a vacuum within the sacred. But God creates that vacuum intentionally, for without it, human growth would be impossible, there would no need for us to work in partnership with God. Order itself would be meaningless, because there would be nothing to measure it against. Without at least a little lust, the ancient rabbis observed, no one would ever have children. It is only in excess that this so-called evil inclination becomes destructive.

Evil becomes a problem when there is an imbalance in the universe. When we follow the model of the Jewish mystics (which I'll explain more fully in chapter 19) and think of the Internet—and everything—as existing within God, when we see these Websites as small clues to God's inner life, what emerges is a noticeable proclivity toward equilibrium. Neither good nor evil can be allowed to expand indefinitely, just as too much justice or too much mercy would upset the careful balance among the divine emanations of the kabbalists. The fact that a good vs. evil Website exists at all shows this inherent need for balance. But within the site there is another proof. Visitors are encouraged to read both the Positive Press and the Daily Outrage and then vote on which one they prefer. "Which had the greater effect on you?" the site asks. "Were you more impressed by the positive qualities shown by the Positive Press or is the Daily Outrage the story that will linger in your mind?" They really want to know, what do people want: people at their best or people at their worst? Good news or bad news?

The tally thus far? Outrageous is leading Positive, 309 to 286. If, out of nearly 600 votes the difference is only 23, the true preference being shown here is neither for good nor evil, but for balance.

If I am to contend that cyberspace has brought us closer to the living God, why not check out a site devoted to one who claimed God is dead and tried to get us "Beyond Good and Evil." Friedrich Nietzsche is also dead, but his pirate page lives on at *www.cwu.edu/~millerj/nietzsche/index.html*. I click a few times, landing on the essay, "Nietzsche and Nihilism," wondering how he would have handled the chaotic mess that would be caused by a dead God. As Dostoyevsky put it, "If God is dead, then nothing is forbidden." I read it with interest, but have no desire to engage dead Nietzsche in an argument over the existence of a living God. The very death of the "God is Dead" movement of the 1960s has done much to resolve that dispute. God has proven remarkably resilient in the face of modernity's unceasing attacks and the breakdown of traditional societies everywhere. God books (and God's books) continue to be bestsellers. Nietszche is comparatively passé. But the essays are interesting. More than the actual content of this site, however, I find remarkable its very existence within the world of the evolving inner God that I believe cyberspace to be. It reminds me of those parts of Yellowstone decimated by fire, where the saplings grow among the charred ruins. The home page of God's death pulsates with divine energy. It is as if God has absorbed nihilism itself and imbued it with meaning.

I can stumble across Nietzsche on my way from Mary Pickford and Thoreau heading toward far more evil sites precisely because God-is-dead has its place in the world of the living God. On this short journey, I've already gone from a hope for individual salvation, espoused in the Pickford quote, to the social liberation dreamt of by Thoreau, to a cold slap in the face presented by a quote from "The Gay Science," "Whither is God? I will tell you. We have killed him—you and I."

No, God is likely not an endangered species, but faith is. Specifically, my faith is. It is a constant struggle for me to maintain the energy—and the degree of hope—to engage in what I perceive to be God's work, every day of my life. On the facade of the ark holding the Torahs of my synagogue's small chapel, there is in Hebrew the inspirational quote from Ps. 16, "I have set the Lord before me always." I would do well to use it as a screen saver, but only if it was accompanied by that quote from Nietzsche. For just as my fate lies in God's hands, God's fate rests in mine.

For just a little reminder of the absurdity of it all, I next visit a site on the AltaVista list, "Bert is Evil." Yes, it seems that we should all keep our children away from that despicable Sesame Street character. Numerous incriminating documents have been accumulated at this site tying Bert to heinous activities. In an interview, best friend Ernie lets us know that after the stage lights dim, geeky Bert becomes a "raging maniac." Allegedly Bert once threatened to kill Rubber Duckie and almost strangled Ernie to death. Bert has experimented with numerous drugs and does unspeakable things to Ernie in the pigeon shed. It all leaves me asking a single question:

Why?

Why is this funny?

I must admit, it is funny to me. It reminds me of the old *Saturday Night Live* skit where Charles Barkley mutilates Barney the dinosaur in a pick-up game of one-on-one. It reminds me of the time I put on a Barney costume during the Jewish festival of Purim, and all the older kids began to beat me up. Barney, who is as squeaky clean as purple dinosaurs go, is so good he's got to be knocked down a peg or two. Over the years, I've seen dozens of Websites that do just that to him. A perfectly balanced universe must include all that is good and its opposite. Cyberspace is as much in balance as a home designed under the principles of feng shui—and this ancient Chinese concept is finding great popularity in the West these days (for a quick summary on how it relates spirituality to space, check out *http://house-craft.com/fengshui.html*).

It's not that good and evil must exist in utter equality in the universe; in fact, my searches of both AltaVista and Excite showed that "good" gets many more hits than "evil," a discrepancy that could increase gradually over time as the presence of God expands. But the presence of Evil Bert and Evil Barney, like the nagging warnings of Nietzsche, though not indications of true evil on the Web, have been good training for me in how to approach that which is far worse, the sites I'm about to visit.

I'm ready now to dive. Let's try *www.evil.com* on a whim. Sure enough, it is there, with some cryptic messages and a paranoiac "we have been infiltrated" warning. "Be warned, there are strangers among us." After that, the site is a tame listing of "top ten" evil links and another list of why *evil.com* exists. (Number seven— "Live is evil spelled backward"; and number eight—"Requested *Elvis.com*, guys at Best messed up"). Enough humor.

I wonder how many supposed evil sites are not really evil at all—and how many are, without calling themselves that. This is the point where I jump off the "evil" search and look in more fertile territory, not where evil says it is, but where it really is: *www.Aryan.com*.

It's there, though I wish I hadn't told you. (Maybe it's not there anymore. I tried to visit it more recently and was unable to make a connection.) The homepage shows, innocently enough, a drawing at the top of a wholesome couple gazing at their cute newborn, but with the ominous caption, "It is a simple reality that . . . to be born WHITE is an honor and a privilege." The next thing you see is the number of hits on that site, 8,929 as of the time I went there. I wonder how many were more impressionable than I. The couple looks so tranquil, so friendly. It reminds me that the Hebrew word for "evil" is almost identical to the word for "friend" (and shepherd, as I mentioned in chapter 1). It can be so deceptive.

So can numbers, and this site is cooked with numbers alleging to show that African Americans (called by less flattering names here) are responsible for almost every social manifestation of evil imaginable, from the transmission of diseases to violent crime. It is a four-page litany of hate. Some of the "facts" go far beyond falsification of truth, they border on incitement: "During the days of slavery a black child was more likely to grow up living with both parents than he or she is today."

I won't argue facts here, just as I didn't argue with Nietzsche. I am not comfortable seeing this garbage on the Web, and now having opened it, seeing it stare at me from my monitor, I wish I could wash my hard drive out with soap. I wish there was some cleansing ritual to eliminate this hate pollution from my sacred space. But it is there, in front of me, closer to me than any such garbage has ever been. I have let it in, and it was so easy. And it looks so normal. There's even an ad on the bottom of the last page, a contest for a free trip for two to Orlando. For what, a lynching?

The site also has a guest list. My synagogue's Website has a guest list, too, one that looks almost identical to this one. No wonder. It *is* identical—from the same company. My first impulse is to call our Webmaster and demand that we change guestbooks. My second reaction is . . . that this might not be so bad after all. If God is the God of good and evil, than even this pure, virulent strain of hate is of God. And somehow it is less dangerous precisely because it is linked to my synagogue by this electronic quirk. I'm upset, but imagine how they would feel if they found out that *Aryan.com* is inexorably linked to Temple Beth El. If Websites were sacred texts, as I believe them to be, this is a perfect example of the rabbinic interpretive category known as *sod,* that hidden meaning of a text that is most true, yet completely divorced from the plain, literal meaning (the *peshat*). After seeing that secret connection between *aryan.com* and *tbe.org,* I am greatly relieved.[36]

And then I begin to read the guests' comments. I only have time to read a dozen or so. All are exceedingly negative, many using language more foul than that employed by the hosts. If *Aryan.com*'s goal is to take advantage of the unbridled freedom offered by the Internet to get their message of hate across, having a guest book might not have been such a bright idea. The very freedom that allows for irresponsible expression is also what reins it in. Hatred and bigotry thrive in an atmosphere of repression. They can't survive in the open market of ideas. "The revealed things belong to us." In the open air, their ideas are fair game. The racists have been trumped.

17

Engraved in Fire, the Letters Soar

Surely the Lord God does nothing without revealing his secret to his servants and prophets.

—Amos 3:7

Behold, My word is like fire.

—Jer. 23:29

*W*hy does God talk to us better through the medium of cyberspace?

1. *The Word arrives from another place.* Martin Buber wrote, "The reality of the holy can only be grasped from the standpoint of mystery." As much as the technology behind the Internet is relatively simple and can be explained, there is still the sense that this communication is being received from "beyond."

2. *The Word is immortal, indelible and comprehensible to all.* It can't be erased. Sure, you can wipe my Internet missives off your screen, but they are still in my hard drive, and in someone else's, and somewhere still in yours. Legend has it that when God inscribed the letters on the Ten Commandments, each letter was engraved in fire so that it went clear through the tablets, and miraculously could be equally intelligible to one reading on the other side. There is an indelible nature to electronic writing. Those computer-generated words are also engraved in fire (electricity) and yet take on a life of their own once released into the world. They can

be read in any font or format, and converted instantly to almost any language, miraculously reversing the curse of Babel with the click of a mouse.

The Talmud tells us of Rabbi Hananiah ben Teradyon, who defied the Romans during the second century by teaching Torah in public at a time when that act was forbidden by law. He was arrested and his death was one of the most horrible imaginable. Wrapped in a Torah scroll, he was placed on a pyre of green brush; fire was set to it and wet wool was placed on his chest to prolong the agony for the greatest amount of time possible. As he was dying, his disciples asked him what he saw, and he soothed them with these immortal words, repeated by Jews throughout the world each Yom Kippur: "I see the parchment burning, but the letters are soaring upward."

With one click of the "send" button, our words take on a life beyond the brief life span of our own hardware—either our body's or our computer's. Sanctified by the fire, burned indelibly into the electronic universe, the letters fly free.

3. *The Word is immaterial.* Unlike a piece of paper or parchment, these words cannot easily be held in your hand. They are dreamlike, hanging before our eyes for an instant, quickly disappearing as we scroll down the page. A good attorney would rest his case by saying: "The evidence is *immaterial,* ladies and gentlemen of the jury. If the evidence is not *material,* therefore it must be *spiritual.* (If the words don't *tear,* they must be a *prayer.)*"

4. *It hearkens us back to the primal mystical experiences of the Prophets.* Check out how various prophets received the

Word in previous eras. Look at Ezekiel, whom some believe to have been on hallucinogens when he had his fantastic vision involving high winds, flash fires and four-winged apparitions. In the midst of it all, he describes wheels, weird gleaming wheels with eyes in them, and then he sees the likeness of the glory of God, blinding and colorful, which fills him with a Divine spirit. After all this, at the end of that first chapter, he begins to receive the Word.

Jewish sages have long referred to this first chapter of Ezekiel as "The Account of the Chariot," and generally encouraged followers not to try to dissect its frenzied imagery. It was considered too dangerous, too raw and mystical, too far removed from human comprehension and too close to pure spiritual oxygen to come near. Yet this chapter formed the foundation for virtually all of later Jewish mysticism. And as we don our sunglasses and stare right into its inner core, we focus in on one word that stands out as the key to the entire strange passage: the Hebrew word *hashmal*. It is found in verses 4 and 27 and nowhere else in the entire Bible.

Verse 4 says:

I looked and beheld a storm-wind coming from the north, a huge cloud with flashing fire and radiance all around it, and at the fire's center something like Hashmal.

What is *hashmal?* If we can answer that question, we can come very close to understanding this primal prophetic experience of the Godhead. What is it that appears in the midst of a great fire that appears to be the source of that radiance? The (Christian) *Oxford Bible* simply translates it as a "gleaming bronze." A well-known Jewish version from the Reform movement translates it as "shining amber," adding in its commentary, "Popular belief ascribed mythical qualities to the resinous substance, for the fire it seemed to emit reminded the ancients of lightning." The Greek Septuagint translates *hashmal* as "electron," and in modern Hebrew it means electricity.

The Talmud discusses *hashmal* in one place only, in Tractate Hagigah, page 13a. There, with clear trepidation, the ancient rabbis contemplate whether one may be allowed to discuss the ancient mystery of this word, or whether it is simply too dangerous. They recount the tale of a child who had expounded on the mysteries of *hashmal,* only to have a fire come forth and consume him. The sages consider banning the book of Ezekiel entirely but then think better of it. Straining to define this highly charged term, Rabbi Judah responds, "Living creatures speaking fire. It is taught: [*hashmal* means], 'At times they are silent, at times they speak.' When the utterance goes forth from the mouth of the Holy One, they are silent [a play on the Hebrew word *hash,* for "silence"], and when the utterance goes not forth from the mouth of the Holy One, they speak [a play on the word *malul,* "speak"]."

Who are these "living creatures" that reside at the center of the fire, those shiny beings that produce the sparks, the circuitry that connects all to God? Are they angels, are they humans . . . or are they computers?

The actual etymology of *hashmal* is as mysterious as the vision it comes from, though it appears to come from the root *hshl,* which means "to shatter." But it is oh-so-tempting for linguistic daredevils like me to look over *hashmal's* shoulders at a Hebrew root that looks so much like it in ancient Hebrew script, *hshv,* "to think." Since one could easily assume that Ezekiel's image of God included the notion of wisdom and insight, it is not unimaginable that the fire's source, the *hashmal,* would be thought itself. In fact, in Ezek. 38:10, Ezekiel uses the term *machashevet,* meaning "thought." The fact that it was part of his vocabulary there lends the possibility that the author had it in mind when transcribing that unfathomable vision in Chapter 1, when the word *hashmal* exploded in his head. For it is almost axiomatic among sacred traditions that the spark at the center of the Divine creative fire is wisdom. "As fire consumes all things," we read in the ancient Hindu text *Srimad Bhagavatam,* "so does the fire of knowledge consume all evil and ignorance." Or, closer to Ezekiel's milieu, in Proverbs: "The Lord by wisdom hath founded the earth; by understanding hath He established the heavens."

Various forms of *machashevet* are found in Jeremiah and the Psalms (as in Ps. 92:5, "God's thoughts are very deep"), but that exact form is found only in Ezekiel. And there is one other linguistic fact of note. *Mechashev* and *hashav* are the modern Hebrew terms for "computer." The difference between either word and *hashmal* is well within the realm of potential scribal error. It's a reach, but remember that the biblical text wasn't frozen in its current form until centuries after it was first written down, and that word, *hashmal,* appears *nowhere else* in the Bible.[37] Could it be that Ezekiel's fantastic vision, one that forms the basis for much of Western mysticism, shares a common etymological root with our own contemporary out-of-box experience?

All of which proves nothing of what either Ezekiel or God intended when handing us the mystery of that vision. But even without the wisdom connection, the *hashmal*-in-fire image tells us everything about the parallels between the ancient experience of prophetic revelation and the modern experience of plugging in and downloading the Word.

How so?

1. *The prophet experiences holiness in the context of electrical illumination.* We turn on our computers, patiently wait out the litany of beeps, grinds and buzzes of circuits in conversation with one another, then we crank up the modem to get online amidst an additional array of sounds and blinking lights.

2. *Mystical insight is received without interruption, with silence, and then the response is made in silence.* Most communication via computer does not allow us to interrupt an incoming message midstream. It appears in its entirety before we can respond. And, once the beeps die down, much like those angelic beings described in the Talmud, we read it in solitude and in silence. And then we respond without interruption from the Other side.

3. *Prophetic insight is cumulative.* We receive an additional component of the Word with every download. And the process of attaining the necessary information to formulate a credible message is often painfully slow. Abraham Joshua Heschel wrote, "Prophetic inspiration may come as a flash, but it is a flash of perpetual light. All inspirations of all Israel's prophets are installments of one revelation. . . . A continuity, an all-embracing meaning, welds into a totality every insight the prophet receives."

Hashmal, that flash of electricity, provides the spark, but we must plod through every bit (and byte) of information we receive to remove from each the nuggets of sacred wisdom that bring us closer to enlightenment. This is true of life in general, where it is possible to find God's presence in the tiniest bit of dust as well as the grandest spectacle of nature. But online, where everything is clearly interconnected, the electricity of the Word shines through even more clearly, though it often takes time for the full picture to become clear. Not only can I feel it in every email exchange, I see it in my random Web-surfing, too—even when I err, such as the time I inadvertently typed in *bethel.org* (instead of my synagogue's *tbe.org*) and ended up at Bethel Church in Santa Clara, California, staring at a nice homey photo of pastor Kenneth Dobson and his wife, Kathy. I decided to stay awhile, spent some time admiring Bethel's fabulous mission statement and potpourri of programs that was, pastorally speaking, to die for. I gained much wisdom during that serendipitous encounter, as I do from almost every stop along each Web-surfing journey I take. Pastor Dobson's shared wisdom has now become part of my unfolding revelation.

Embedded within four letters of the Hebrew *hashmal* is the word *shem,* "Name," which is often used by Jews as a pseudonym for God. *Hashmal* is that center, the core source of electricity, which contains God's name, opening windows for the light to shine in. Our computers should all have a decal saying, *"hashmal* inside*"*—except that the *Hashmal* is inside us as well. Without my trusty computer, there is very little in this world that could have linked me to Pastor Kenneth Dobson. We may never speak or meet, on- or off-line, but it no longer matters. We have been linked together eternally in a single grinding, buzzing, beeping, byte-pouring flash; a flash of the revealed Word. We are all linked by a spark of divinity that sets off a chain reaction of relationship, and that takes our mundane words and enables the letters to fly free.

There is one more reason why it would appear natural for God to communicate most clearly through cyberspace, one that will require some additional background explanation:

God is digital.

18

The Second Journey Beyond Good and Evil: Revealing the Hidden Things

Defeating the Darkness

Though I walk through the valley of the shadow of death, I fear no harm, for you are with me.

—Ps. 23:4

Had I not the belief that I would enjoy the goodness of the Lord in the land of the living!

—Ps. 27:13 (a moment of dramatic uncertainty for a poet edging closer to the abyss of despair)

I need to see more hate sites and gauge their impact. I check out the Anti-Defamation League to gain some insight (*www.adl.org*). Here I can read firsthand the accusations of Louis Farrakhan of Jewish involvement in the slave trade and the truth about the "Protocols of the Elders of Zion," that nineteenth-century hoax about Jewish aims for world domination (turns out it was lifted from a nineteenth-century French satire in which the protagonists weren't even Jewish).

I direct my attention to a group being exposed here called the Neo-Nazi National Alliance (NA), considered by the ADL to be "the single most dangerous organized hate group in the United States today." I go on to read how the NA sprang to national attention several years ago, when it was discovered that a fictitious incident in *The Turner Diaries*, a violent and racist novel written by the NA's leader, might have been used as a model for the Oklahoma City bombing. Convicted bomber Timothy McVeigh was a devoted reader of *The Turner Diaries*, which features a bombing scenario that is eerily reminiscent of the April 19, 1995, blast.

The report continues:

> *Like other hate groups today, the National Alliance uses the Internet to showcase its racist and neo-Nazi*

ideology. Group leader William Pierce, who has a doctorate in physics, was quick to understand the potential power of the Internet and to take aggressive steps to incorporate it into the National Alliance propaganda arsenal. The organization relies on the Internet as a tool for recruitment and for broad, inexpensive dissemination of its hate-filled ideas.

The NA maintains one of the most technically sophisticated hate sites on the World Wide Web. Constantly updated, the site effectively uses the idea of "Internet radio." The NA's weekly half-hour American Dissident Voices (ADV) radio broadcasts—transmitted over nine AM or FM radio stations and on shortwave radio via WRNO (based in Metairie, Louisiana)—appear on the group's Website on the day of the broadcast. They then stay in the Website's program archives for several months, ready to be listened to at any time, anywhere in the world. The user simply needs to click a mouse to listen to the violent, hate-filled fantasies of William Pierce, and the venom he aims at Blacks, Jews and other minorities.

In one broadcast, Pierce accused Russian Jewish immigrants in the United States of belonging to a global criminal organization. In another, he railed, "What can we do to free ourselves from the Jews? What can we do to break their death grip on our mass media of news and entertainment and on our political system? How can we bring about an end to their racket of using us to extort money from the rest of the world for them?"

Not surprisingly, the ADL Website offers no help to those who want to log onto this hate site directly. Nor do they assist in gaining direct access to the messages of several other hate groups mentioned in their site. It doesn't matter. I run a quick search. Within three minutes, I am looking directly at the home page of the National Alliance.

"Free speech online," it says, with a little blue ribbon alongside, signaling a "blue ribbon" campaign. At first glance I thought it was an AIDS ribbon. Wrong.

The pale yellow background and royal blue print make for an unimposing, inviting home page. Nothing evil-looking about it, though it does have a smattering of black borders and highlighters. The motto: "Toward a New Consciousness, a New Order, a New People." Everything seems so friendly. There is an address at the bottom of the page, a place in West Virginia—indicating no overt paranoia of being discovered by the authorities. They invite response and print readers' letters. I jump to that page. Unlike the Aryans, they edit their responses, and the result is that they print only supportive mail, with very few exceptions. And so their home-grown trash is augmented by supportive messages from abroad, like this from a certain ZS: "What Dr. Pierce is trying to accomplish involves neither evil nor ignorance. He is giving a wakeup call to White Americans about how we are being used by Jews to serve their clandestine agenda of greed and degeneracy."

I peruse an article about how the Jews control the media. It occurs to me as I finish reading it that the Internet is the only form of mass communication this side of the pager that Pierce doesn't think the Jews control. No one owns the Internet. It is too expansive and unwieldy, I suppose, for any human agent to dominate, even ones as "devious" as the Jews. He must feel so free to patrol the gutters of cyberspace. More articles can be found in dozens of archived issues of the group's periodicals. I figure that there are likely more words on this hate site alone than Goebbels published in his lifetime. If I were at all insecure about my place in the country my family has called home for four generations, I'd be petrified.

But where would I move? These lies know no national bounds. They appear here in several languages, especially Swedish, Dutch and German. National borders have little meaning on the Internet. The site contains lots of archived broadcasts. I can't bring myself to listen to any.

I'm very tired and confused. How can God be part of all this? How can the proliferation of this garbage possibly help advance the defeat of evil? How can this be a necessary complement to the good? It's just past midnight and I'm calling into question my whole enterprise, this whole book. Could there really be that much hatred out there? Do that many people see me as trying to undermine the country I love? Visions of right-wing conspiracies dance in my head. Those, and that image of the fireman carrying out the baby after the Oklahoma City bombing. The man who inspired that act of terror is still at it, and doing his thing on the very thing I've been claiming is an instrument for prophecy. Then I think of those preschoolers at the Jewish Community Center near Los Angeles, terrorized by a hate-monger seeking to deliver a "wake-up call" to Americans to kill Jews. Just as the doctor (Pierce) ordered.

After thoroughly investigating reams of material at this site, I quickly scan a couple of similar, though less substantial, hate sites (including *www.kkk.com*, complete with white hoods and burning crosses), then decide to sleep this off.

But I can't sleep. I'm too busy fighting the darkness. My mind is stirred by the sleepless nights of victims of hate. My life's work has been directed toward defeating the darkness, but the darkness seems so overwhelming now, its tentacles so long and free to do their bidding. As a rabbi, I've become trapped in a sugarcoated world, proclaiming the light of faith, denying doubt, suppressing my own doubt, in order to lift up others. But this night I am stricken by fear, my eyes are paralyzed open.

19

The Digital God

And He created His universe
  with three books [Sepharim]
  with text [Sepher]
  with number [Sephar]
  and with communication (Sippur).

—*Sefer Yetzira (The Book of Creation)*
  c. sixth century kabbalistic work[38]

T hus far we've tracked God online through the rediscovery of lost parents and through imagery like the web, the word and electrical illumination. Now picture if you will God as a tree. True, "the Lord is My Tree" is hardly a romantic notion. Want romance? How about God as a human body, one with both male and female gentalia? Too risqué? Then how about God as a labyrinth of letters? A hand? A wheel of light? Candles in a mirror?

What all of these metaphors have in common is that they are forms that have been utilized to depict the stages of God's "development" according to the Jewish mystical theological system known as kabbalah (Hebrew for "that which is received or revealed"). These poetic images all play off of a basic kabbalistic concept, one that resonates remarkably within our computerized culture. It is the notion of the ten *Sefirot,* or emanations, of God.

God as a Work-in-Progress

To understand the *Sefirot,* you must first embrace the presupposition that God is a work-in-progress. Our postmodern view of the universe as something ever-unfolding and expanding is analogous to the kabbalistic view of God. Creation didn't just happen—it is still happening. God wasn't just "there" to order everything into existence; aspects of

God themselves emanated from a primal source, on a higher plane of reality, eventually enabling all that appears real in our material world to take shape. God isn't so much a "Supreme Being" as an ever-evolving conglomeration of all of these stages of emanation.[39]

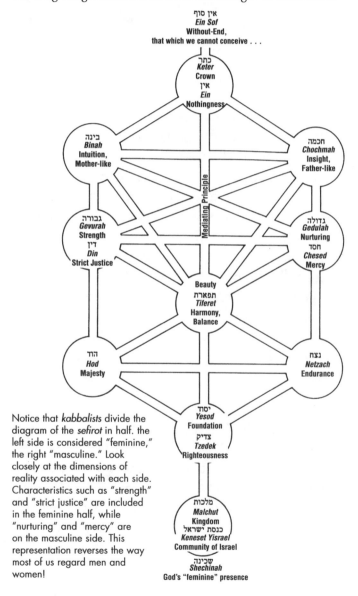

אין סוף
Ein Sof
Without-End,
that which we cannot conceive . . .

כתר
Keter
Crown
אין
Ein
Nothingness

בינה
Binah
Intuition,
Mother-like

חכמה
Chochmah
Insight,
Father-like

Mediating Principle

גבורה
Gevurah
Strength
דין
Din
Strict Justice

גדולה
Gedulah
Nurturing
חסד
Chesed
Mercy

Beauty
תפארת
Tiferet
Harmony,
Balance

הוד
Hod
Majesty

נצח
Netzach
Endurance

יסוד
Yesod
Foundation
צדיק
Tzedek
Righteousness

מלכות
Malchut
Kingdom
כנסת ישראל
Keneset Yisrael
Community of Israel
שכינה
Shechinah
God's "feminine" presence

Notice that *kabbalists* divide the diagram of the *sefirot* in half. the left side is considered "feminine," the right "masculine." Look closely at the dimensions of reality associated with each side. Characteristics such as "strength" and "strict justice" are included in the feminine half, while "nurturing" and "mercy" are on the masculine side. This representation reverses the way most of us regard men and women!

Professor Gershom Scholem, a great modern interpreter of kabbalah, compares these emanations to a candle flickering in the midst of
ten mirrors set one within the other, with each mirror being a different
color."[40] Mere humans can never "see" all of God, but as God's light is
refracted through these mirrors, each of these emanations points to an
aspect of God that can be discerned by those who are most wise and
perceptive. This unfolding creation begins with a single "candle," not
perceivable to human beings, known as *Einsof* (the Infinite). From this
emerge the ten *Sefirot*, whose names all derive from the Bible. First is
Keter (crown), representing the first "flash" of thought, that spark of
divine will that precedes actual thought in the process of creation.
Then comes *Chochmah* (wisdom) and *Binah* (understanding), often seen
as a pair. While each speaks of the process of thinking and planning,
the creating of a divine "blueprint" for creation, *Chochmah* is often associated with masculinity, as the beginning of thought, and *Binah* with
feminine imagery, as the womb in which the creative plan is implanted
and the wellspring from which it emerges.

Confused yet? I hope so, because even great sages have lost their
sanity contemplating such deep thoughts. Traditionally, even the wis-
est scholar isn't supposed to embark upon kabbalistic speculation until
after reaching the age of forty. When you consider it, the idea of a
male/female God gestating the universe is actually rather more plau-
sible than the idea of God as the great-detached stage manager, as the
book of Genesis would seem to have it. We're not finished yet, though,
so hang on.

Chochmah and *Binah* give rise to the next two emanations, *Chesed* and
Din, mercy and justice. These, too, have sexual associations, but not in
the way our knee-jerk gender stereotypes would lead us to assume:
Justice is seen as a feminine attribute and mercy as masculine. Both
exist within God, and therefore within the universe and within each of
us. The key, from a kabbalistic standpoint, is that they must coexist in

absolute balance. With too much justice and not enough mercy, rigidity will reign, an imbalance that a kabbalist might see as the root of evil. On the other hand, with too much love and not enough justice, without set boundaries and limits, there can be no growth. From this perspective, the questions we face each day—with coworkers, with family and within ourselves, as we seek that precious balance between rigidity and flexibility, between justice and mercy—are at the core of what holds the very universe in balance.

Din and *Chesed* give birth to the emanation of *Tiferet*, beauty. When we read of the Lord in the Bible (when the name is spelled out using the Hebrew letters *yod-heh-vav-heh*, also known as the tetragrammaton), kabbalists see this as the emanation of *Tiferet* breaking through. Because it is the synthesis, the "child," of *Din* and *Chesed*, justice and mercy flow through *Tiferet* in perfect harmony. Then come another matched pair, *Hod* and *Netzach*, "majesty" and "victory." These are the emanations of justice and mercy as filtered through *Tiferet*, not perfectly pure, but far better suited to govern the natural order of the universe. Just as the air we breathe isn't pure oxygen, neither are the love and justice we experience on earth pure *Din* and *Chesed*.

Finally there are *Yesod*, foundation, often symbolized by the phallus, which ensures procreation within the material world, and *Malchut*, also known as *Shechinah*, *Yesod's* female partner in this divine chain of being. There we have the ten emanations of divinity, the *Sefirot*.

We've come light years from "The Lord is my Shepherd," haven't we? Here we see God not as Supreme Being but rather as a system, a life process, an eternal dialectic, analogous to the yin/yang of Chinese traditions. The parallels between the Sefirot and Chinese religion are even more striking when we look at the teachings of Lao-tzu's classic *Tao Te Ching* translated by Stephen Mitchell[41]:

The tao [teaching] that can be told
is not the eternal Tao.
The name that can be named
Is not the eternal Name.
The unnamable is the eternally real.
Yet mystery and manifestations
arise from the same source.

Sounds just like the kabbalistic *Ein Sof,* complete with emanations. Lao-tzu's ideal character is a person in perfect harmony with himself:

The kind man does something;
yet something remains undone.
The just man does something,
And leaves many things to be done . . .
The Master does nothing
Yet he leaves nothing undone.

That balance between justice and mercy, which Lao-tzu finds only in the ideal human, is something that kabbalah finds in that complicated ecosystem that we call God. God is both good and evil, male and female, sexual yet sexless. In Scholem's words, "The rhythm of the unfolding *Sefirot* is the fundamental rhythm of all creation." kabbalistic speculation is all very complicated and has been revised often over the centuries. For our purposes, what we need to remember is the following:

1. *The divine qualities of the* Sefirot *also exist within us:* We are the microcosm of God's macrocosm. All that is out *there* is also in *here.* We are part of the divine system. We participate in the life of God!

Later kabbalistic theory takes that quite literally, positing that with every divine commandment we fulfill, as we balance the chaotic forces within us, we are helping to "complete" God, and to make the universe perfect, harmonious and whole.

2. *These emanations are all interconnected, creating a dynamic Unity.* They feed off of each other. According to the increasingly popular "Gaia Hypothesis," the universe is one vast organism, just like our bodies and our communities, and like the earth itself. kabbalists have shown this through the use of metaphors like the tree, human body and spoked wheel of light.

3. *They exist in balance.* Without equilibrium, the entire universe is at risk of collapsing into chaos.

4. *Reality is unfolding.* Like these divine emanations, the fundamental truths of the universe are presenting themselves to us bit by bit, with each passing moment.

5. *This unfolding is best understood through sexual imagery.* We're not talking about dirty pictures here, which abound on the Internet. What I'm saying is that the way we come to deepen our relationship with the divine through kabbalistic glasses is to measure the ebb and flow of creation in terms of the balance of male and female qualities in the universe. Sexual harmony is divine harmony.

Once again we find parallels in *Tao te Ching,* written at least eight centuries before (and half a world away from) Sefer Yetzira:

> All things have their backs to the female
> and stand facing the male.
> When male and female combine,
> All things achieve harmony.

In a sense we *are* talking about those dirty Websites here, as an example of what happens when there is an imbalance between the divine qualities of *Chesed* and *Din*. When sexual expression goes unrestrained, when there are no boundaries set and permissiveness reigns, when male-female harmony is disrupted, the results are found in the XXX section of your friendly Web browser. We'll take a closer look at this in a later segment of this book.

You might have guessed from the above comment that I am about to plug the Internet and specifically the Web into this kabbalistic divine system. I am, but first I need to explain one more very important aspect of the *Sefirot*.

6. The *Sefirot* are digital. Okay, now I *know* you're lost. The system of the *Sefirot* so perfectly aligns itself to our postmodern age not only because it presupposes an expanding, dynamic creation, and not only because it is all about drawing connections and seeking equilibrium. The *Sefirot* plug right into our P.C.s because in this system of conceptualizing God, much like our system of understanding computers, *letters and numbers are the building blocks of Reality.*

0s and 1s

Previously I've explored the famous verse from the Gospel of John. "In the beginning, there was the Word." In truth, there were a number of words in the beginning: to be precise, there were ten occasions in the Creation account of Gen. 1 when God spoke a creative command (actually nine, plus the initial, not-specifically-verbal act of Gen. 1:1, "In the beginning, God *created* . . ."). Early kabbalists looked closely at these utterances, from "Let there be light" on the first day to "Be fruitful and multiply" on the sixth, and from this they derived the concept of ten *Sefirot*. The term *Sefirot* itself comes from the Hebrew term meaning "number." In addition to these utterances, God's name appears twenty-two other times in that Creation account, such as when the text says, "God *saw* that it was good." There happen to be twenty-two letters in the Hebrew alphabet. So let's see. Ten utterances, ten digits; twenty-two other depictions of God, twenty-two letters. Coincidence? Speaking kabbalistically, I don't think so.

At least the author of *Sefer Yetzirah,* the *Book of Creation,* who lived around the sixth century, didn't think so. This seminal mystical tract begins, "With thirty-two mystical paths of Wisdom . . . He created the Universe; with three books, with text, with number and with communication." The Hebrew words for text and book *(sefer),* number *(sefar* or *mispar)* and communication and story *(sippur)* are almost identical, so a connection is made instantly.

It is important to note that each Hebrew letter has a numerical equivalent. For example, *alef,* the first letter, corresponds to the number one, and *yod,* the tenth letter, equals ten. Once we go beyond ten, the letters take on values of multiples of ten *(lamed* is 30 and *mem,* the next letter, equals 40), and then 100 *(kuf* is 100 and the next letter, *resh,* equals 200), until the last letter, *tav,* carries with it the numerical value of 400. With letters and numbers interchangeable, it is common to see quantities expressed alphabetically: Jewish years and dates, even holidays, are often described using letters rather than numbers. The Jewish Arbor Day, for instance, is called *Tu B'Shevat. Shevat* is the name of the month in which it falls (usually around the beginning of February), and *Tu* is the date, the fifteenth. Why the fifteenth? Because the Hebrew letters *tet* (9) and *vav* (6) when added together equal fifteen, and when placed together those two letters spell out the word *"Tu."* (The reason we don't add ten and five, which would seem more logical, is because the letters *yod* [10] and *heh* [5], when placed together, spell out a version of God's name [*Yah*], a name Jews are commanded not to utter in vain.)

One popular kabbalistic exercise is to use numerical values of words to decipher hidden meanings in a sacred text. I've already done that in this book, at the end of chapter five, when I showed the equivalence of the words for "one" and "love" (both equal 13) and their relationship to God's name (which equals 26, the sum of unity and love).

The interconnection of letters and numbers is not unique to Jewish culture. Numbers have been plumbed for deeper meaning in world culture at least since Pythagoras, who said that all things could be traced back to numbers, especially in relation to geometric patterns. On the other side of the globe, Lao-tzu also got digital about the generative nature of Reality:

> *The Tao gives birth to One.*
> *One gives birth to Two.*
> *Two gives birth to Three*
> *Three gives birth to all things.*

Numerology has most recently become a New Age staple, and decoding numerological Bible codes a bestselling pastime.

Where does this leave us? In the words of Rabbi Aryeh Kaplan, a contemporary kabbalist and translator of *Sefer Yetzirah,* "The letters and digits are the basis of the most basic ingredients of creation, quality and quantity. The qualities of any given thing can be described by words formed out of the letters, while all of its associated quantities can be expressed in numbers." This is put more simply in Eccles. 11:21: "Thou hast ordered all things in measure and number and weight." There is a numerical basis to that which brings order from chaos.

And there is a numerical basis to Creation as it is made manifest to us online.

The digital nature of computer language is known to anyone who has studied how a computer works, meaning most people younger than me. If I am a self-proclaimed member of the younger generation regarding theology (in that the shepherd metaphor doesn't work for me as it did for my parents), the same cannot be said in respect to computer science, where I'm downright ancient. When I was in high school, we did have computer classes, but I was too busy learning other, supposedly more relevant things. I did go down to the computer room from time to time. It was called the computer room not because there were computers in the room, but because the computer—the only computer—took up most of the room. I observed, with scant interest, as classmates tried to program the computer using punched-out cards with numbers on them. But I wasn't so apathetic as to disregard the fundamental significance of numbers.

The numbers are interesting. What's more interesting is how computer language evolves, dare I say emanates, until at last it reaches our screens and is accessible to us Neanderthal "dummies." The building blocks are those combinations of 0s and 1s known as "Machine Code," the only language computers understand. As my computer itself informed me (through Microsoft *Encarta,* a multimedia encyclopedia), "all other programming languages represent ways of structuring human language so that humans can get computers to perform specific tasks." It begins with the basic language of numbers, which beget letters, which begets language, which begets comprehensible meaning. It all starts with the numbers.

In the simplest terms, *a computer is simply a box of switches that are either off or on, and the switches are represented by the numbers 0 and 1.*[42]

If the author of *Sefer Yetzirah* were alive today, he would see the computer screen as a window to Creation, a mirror reflecting the essence of the godhead. I doubt Bill Gates had this in mind when he opted to utilize the window metaphor in naming his product, but that's exactly what it is. The computer, through its software, is a prism, refracting and distilling the most basic codes of reality, the 0s and 1s, and translating them into some semblance of meaning and order for us. The numbers are too elemental, too pure, too far beyond us to comprehend and decipher; they are direct products of the *Ein Sof,* by way of *Chochmah* and

Binah. But by the time we see this information as distilled through Windows (or an equivalent), through emanations closer to human comprehension, we can begin to comprehend the truth. "Windows" therefore serves much the same function as the divine emanation of *Tiferet,* which helps filter out that which is beyond our ken.

Does this make Bill Gates a messenger of God? No. He's more of a translator, an oracle. Otherwise, he is, like each of us, a participant in the life of God, a tiny blip in the divine drama of forging order from chaos, a drama unfolding both on and off our screens.

But wait a minute! Just because a computer's reality begins with 0s and 1s and the kabbalistic godhead happens also to be digital, does that really allow me to take such a leap of faith as to say that the world of cyberspace is a reflection of God's inner life?

I questioned that too, until my own research brought me deeper and deeper into the subject. My next step was to look more closely at those basic elements of digital reality, the 0s and the 1s.

The Face of the Waters

But first, some reflections on surfing.

If we are to see the Web as a kabbalist would, the first thing we've got to do is stop surfing. We typically think of surfing as skimming the surface of a wave with the objective of staying dry, and that's hardly what we're doing when we are seeking God in any context, whether online, at religious services or anywhere we seek spirituality. The experience of the sacred must, above all, be one that deepens us and puts us in touch with the Source of all being and existence. Surfing implies superficiality and diversion from what is real and important. That might be what we do in Malibu or Waikiki, but when we go online we aren't skimming, we're *diving,* plumbing the depths until we reach the purest possible glimpse of Reality, that which is closest to the Source.

A well-trained kabbalist might occasionally recognize glimpses of those more distant, undistilled *Sefirot,* by decoding secrets embedded within sacred text.

But diving the Net, like all aquatic activity, does require that we come up for air occasionally. We can't exist solely beneath the surface, even though that's where much meaning can be found. God exists both above and below. When we read in Gen. 1, "And the spirit of God moved upon the face of the waters," we can begin to understand the dynamic, flowing nature of that Spirit, and that in order to encounter it, we can't be afraid to get wet. True, it's dangerous to submerge; that's why kabbalah is not for the neophyte. The greatest danger is that we might be unable to come up.

From time immemorial, the surface of the water has been a locus for profound religious experience encounter. Moses means "taken from the water," and the epochal events of his birth and his people's salvation revolved around the sea. The Hindu gods Brahma and Vishnu each carry the name *Narayana,* "He who walks on the waters"; and another appellation given Brahma is *Apava,* "He who sports on the waters." Eastern traditions are replete with imagery of the lotus, a sacred flower that reposes upon the water and opens to the sunlight. That unfolding is considered a perfect expression of peace and a step toward the realization of spiritual possibilities. Jesus walked on the waters of Galilee, and the Quran teaches that Allah's "throne was upon the water." The ever-changing surface of the water, a penetrable mirror, separates worlds that are equally real, and without that separation, equally chaotic. The existence of the surface itself establishes order. It is a boundary between the world above and the world below.

The world of the Internet is that world below. If we are surfing it, then we are riding upside down, with our bodies submerged but maintaining contact with the undercurrent of the wave. More like dolphins than human beings, we dive and leap, above and below, repeatedly penetrating the Face of the Waters, gazing at that constantly shifting Spirit from above and beneath. When we dare, and when we are able, we dive deeper.

20

The Second Journey
Beyond Good and Evil:
Revealing the Hidden Things

Justice and Mercy:
Establishing Divine Order

Come, let us return to the Lord,
For He has torn, that He may heal us;
He has stricken and He will bind us up.

—Hos. 6:1

*T*he next day, again late at night, I plod on, back to the ADL site, where I read that "hundreds upon hundreds" of Websites promote a variety of hateful philosophies. Among the newest strain: "Hateful Women on the Web."

"While bigots often target women, some women have themselves become bigots, spewing hate on the Internet aimed at Jews, blacks and other minorities. Many female-oriented hate sites publish extremist creeds similar to those at man-made sites, but hateful women are using the Internet primarily as a tool to promote discussion of their role in the white supremacist 'movement.'"

I try to log onto one such site, the "World Church of the Creator," but end up instead at the site for another Church of the Creator, in Portland, Oregon. At first I'm relieved at having stumbled upon what appears a nice, tolerant interfaith organization, until I read its creed. The goal is unification and oneness of all humankind. That's nice—it's my goal too (and what, as I have stated, the Internet is helping to accomplish), and they want to "join harmoniously in oneness . . . bringing forth by example to this planet earth love, light and peace; therefore decreeing DIVINE RIGHT ORDER in all thoughts, all things, our universe automatically aligns into a manifestation of heaven on earth." This is all to be done through the priesthood of Mechizedek and "in the body of Jesus Christ."

There is no hate here, only love and peace and order and unity, all the things I've ever preached—including what I've been talking about in this book. And these are the very things endorsed by the hate groups. While this is very different from the hate sites I've encountered, it is equally threatening to me, because this group's definition of unity requires that I capitulate to its vision. Does this make for hate, or supreme love?

I reflect that not only are the Hebrew words for "evil" and "friend" virtually identical, but that it is also the same as the word for "shepherd" and for "decree." Is this God's evil decree? Is this the last desperate act of the Shepherd, before that divine metaphor is put out to pasture? Are all lines to be blurred, so that in the end the only difference between what is good and what is hateful will be that if it is done by me it is good and if it is done to me it is hateful? I feel that Nietzsche is somehow dragging at my heels, pulling me back toward his brand of moral relativism and away from the ethical certainty I had once thought possible. I, like most others, need to see that line clearly, the one separating good from evil. I need to affirm the knowledge gained from eating that tree in the Garden.

I reflect on a verse from the Jewish evening liturgy, praising God for distinguishing between darkness and light. Note how the wording of this prayer specifically states that it is God who distinguishes between day and night, not us. It is God who creates light and darkness, good and evil, and it is God who ultimately knows the difference. We might have eaten the fruit of that tree in the Garden, but we haven't quite digested it yet. When we look at day and night, we primarily see dawn and dusk. The line between what is good and what is evil is one of those secret things that belong to God. But the line does exist. There is a definable, objective truth out there. We just can't know it for certain.

And that is precisely what makes the Church of the Creator an example of what one could call evil. The believers behind that site are certain. They claim to be filled with love and mercy, but it is merely a mask for what is actually an imbalance toward the divine quality of justice *(din)* in its purest and most dangerous form. Justice unchecked leads to self-righteousness and blinds us to the complexity and ultimate unknowability of truth and of God. It forces us to see our neighbor not as a fellow human being with the right to autonomous beliefs, but as a pawn ready to be taken and used for our purposes, an object, an "it." Love, but only on my terms, is tough love indeed; it is not really love at all.

We can't find God in places that claim to know God. That's pure *din.*

We can't find God in places that accept all views equally, even when those views justify unspeakable and unpardonable acts. That's an example of unmitigated *Chesed* (mercy). While the acts of the hate group hardly sound merciful, when they plead for their free speech (and therefore the freedom to incite), they are playing on a basic universal desire for tolerance. They are taking advantage of our *hesed,* our good will and pluralistic nature, to bring about a world that would ultimately be devoid of both mercy and justice.

So the missionary group and the hate group each expose a basic imbalance in the cyber universe that is the inner life of God. That is what makes them "evil." That is why our job is to restore balance, by adding the boundaries of "justice" where necessary in curbing the impact of online incitement (though not by restricting free speech), and by adding the freedom of "mercy" by teaching true tolerance to those groups who claim to have a monopoly on God's truth.

My stumbling upon the missionary group was a fortuitous accident; I decide to forego female hate groups and dive into the darkness some more, this time not to find hate, zealotry or cynicism, but lust.

21

The Alef and "I"

T he voice of the Lord divides the
   flames of fire.
The voice of the Lord convulses
   the wilderness.

—Ps. 29

T he Great Shofar is sounded;
a still small voice is heard.

—High Holy Days liturgy

One afternoon I was contemplating the basic elements of digital reality, those combinations of 0s and 1s, and what they could teach us about the digital nature of God. So I splashed and dove to a Jewish numerology Website (*www.inner.org/HEBLETER/alef.htm*). There I clicked on the letter *alef*.[43]

Alef, the first letter of the Hebrew alphabet, equals one in Hebrew numerology and is the first letter in the word meaning "one," *ehad*. It is also the first letter of the word *efes*, which means zero and *ayn*, which means nothing. Since no other letter by itself equals zero in the numerological system, the paradox of *alef* is that it equals both oneness and nothingness simultaneously. If we were to look for letters with which to duplicate the basic pattern of digital reality, the 1s and 0s, we would end up with only *alef*s.

This unusual letter is perfectly suited to such a paradoxical role, for the *alef* is one letter with zero sound. It is unutterable when it stands by itself. Hebrew has one other silent letter, *ayin*, a letter that some kabbalists also equate with zero, but in truth *ayin* can be pronounced, although with great difficulty for Westerners, as a guttural, almost choking sound from the back of the throat. Not so *alef*. Jewish mystics have long seen the *alef* as the sound that occurs just as sound is beginning, the utterance before there is utterance. The first word of the Ten Commandments begins with *alef,* in Hebrew *Anochi,* which is a formal way of saying "I."

> *"I am the Lord your God who brought you out of the Land of Egypt." (Exod. 20:1)*

The Bible tells us that when the Israelites saw the mountain smoking and quaking and heard the thunder and flames and the sound of the ram's horn, they trembled and begged Moses to speak to them in God's stead. Moses did just that, interpreting those fateful commands, allowing the divine will to be distilled through a human interpolator. It was as if God's direct communication was too pure to be understood and too awesome to contemplate. In kabbalistic terms, the Commandments needed to be filtered through more accessible emanations. God's word needed to become more user-friendly.

But tradition would have us believe that God and Israel forged a covenant at Sinai, and for that to happen Israel would have had to have heard at least something of God's word directly. If the whole thing had been filtered through Moses, that covenant would have been cheapened considerably. The entire enterprise would have been cast into doubt. Israel's acceptance of divine will could not be based on hearsay. Yet the text appears to be telling us that God's word was received secondhand.

The ancient rabbinic commentators had an ingenious

way to get around this problem. Moses repeated virtually all of the Ten Commandments to the people, they said, all except one letter. The very first letter of the very first word was spoken directly by God to the 600,000 or so Israelites who stood alongside the mountain. And that letter was the silent *alef,* the *alef* of *anochi,* the " " of "I."

The people heard nothing (think of what you say as you begin to pronounce the word "I"), but they heard everything. The paradox of *alef* is that it can be nothing and everything at the same time. *Hearing that* alef *in our day would be that experience of hearing computers speak to one another, in that deafening whir of nothingness, of 1s and 0s in incalculable patterns.* We can take it only for a second, after which we ask Bill Gates to translate it for us.

To summarize: The *alef,* that letter that speaks in "computer language" of unintelligible ones and zeros, was the only letter that God actually uttered directly to humanity at the one time when large numbers of people actually heard God. The Revelation at Sinai could in fact be seen as a *digital* Revelation, just as the Creation was digital. Does it take a huge leap of faith, then, to see the digital communications of our age as in fact a return to a more basic, and even direct form of divine-human interaction?

Two Surfers—One Board

But there's more to the *alef* than its numerical/digital equivalent. The letter *alef* is formed by two *yods,* one to the upper right and one to the lower left, joined by a diagonal *vav.* These two letters, nearly silent themselves, comprise half of the tetragrammaton. If you look closely at the letter *alef* (see the diagram), and find these other letters there, it doesn't take a whole lot of imagination to envision the two *yod*s as surfing on a *vav*-shaped board, with one *yod* above the surface of the water and the other beneath it.

The Letter *Alef*

The Letters *Yod* and *Vav*

These two *yod*s and *vav* represent the higher and lower waters and the firmament between them, according to the teachings of Rabbi Isaac Luria, a towering kabbalistic master of the sixteenth century. At the time of Creation, when God's spirit hovered over the surface of the waters, the higher waters and lower waters were indistinguishable. On the second day of Creation, God separated the two waters by stretching the firmament between them. The letter *alef* therefore is an "artist's depiction" of that great moment of separation.

The Website I referred to at the beginning of this chapter explains this depiction as follows: "In Jewish philosophy, two intrinsic properties of water are 'wet' and 'cold.' The higher water is 'wet' with the feeling of oneness . . . while the lower water is 'cold' with the feeling of separation, the experience of being far from God."

The *alef* possesses the unique ability to connect the waters above and below, with that *vav* separating and uniting them simultaneously. The *alef* straddles the surface, just like we do, allowing us to become one with God at times, and leaving us feeling spiritually empty and cold at others. How like our own experience is this alternating push and pull of alienation and connectedness; and how elemental to the human predicament it is. Only through God can the higher and lower waters be locked in place in perfect balance.

We live in two worlds, that of the flesh and that of the digit. Which one is more real? They both are real, but from the kabbalistic perspective, reality is digital at its most basic essence. All worlds, those of material and those of the spirit, those of being and those of nothingness, those of unity and those of separation, are united by a single letter-turned-digit, the *alef* of "I," the *alef* of 1s and 0s, the *alef,* best approximated by the inflection of a computer, the *alef* viewed by tradition as the inaudibly perceptible voice of God.

22

The Second Journey
Beyond Good and Evil:
Revealing the Hidden Things

The Hidden Things Revealed

Look to the Lord;
be strong and of good courage!
O, look to the Lord.

—Ps. 27:14 (responding to his despair, acknowledged
in the previous verse, the psalmist carries on despite all doubts,
affirming order in the midst of the chaos around him)

Smut is not hard to find on the Web. All I had to do, actually, was type in *www.sin.com.* If you have children, please blacken that out. But don't expect that they won't find it eventually, even with the best filters and childproofing. It's there, and more accessible than ever. Much as we might want to, we just don't live in the Summer of 1942 anymore, where upstanding drugstore owners could keep inappropriate materials out of the hands of our kids. I don't make it my business to dwell in X-rated neighborhoods, but this survey would be incomplete without a brief visit to the red-light district of the Net.

I won't go into detail, but it's all there. If you wish, your desktop can in seconds become Sodom and Gomorrah. So can your public library, your office, your child's classroom, the Oval Office. It's all there, in plain view. The site I randomly selected offers a link to live sex from Amsterdam. Interesting, because I was just thinking about Amsterdam when I saw the first vixen welcoming me to the site. I recalled the thoughts I had when strolling through that city's famed red-light district years ago. The first thing I noticed was that it actually had red lights, and how similar they were in principle to the lights on top of New York taxicabs. When the light is on, there's a vacancy. My second impression was how run-down and decrepit the area looked, and the women, too, equally worn and sleepy-eyed. Depressing. I felt badly for them, as one does for a homeless person on a city street. "Whose daughter are you?" I wished to ask. "Here, cover yourself. How can I get you back home?"

Sexuality is not in itself evil. I can imagine loving, married couples making great use of adult Websites, much as they do with adult videos. I'm also not so certain that the accessibility of Internet sex sites will lead our children to lives of depravity. The impact of the site I visited was neither titillation nor disgust, but a yawn. When I looked at it, I felt sad, as I did in Amsterdam, that people have to sell their bodies to gain self-worth. But the hard fact is that, once the clothes are off, there is little left that is sexy. What's sexy is the anticipation, the unfolding and the emotional attachment— the love. Unwrapping a Torah scroll is sexy. Hindu temple art is sexy. When you click on a Website and everyone is already naked and having at it, one can hardly call it sexy, evil, tempting or anything else but just plain boring.

I've never been a great fan of permissiveness. I can recall visiting a girlfriend when I was a teen in the early 1970s and being told that her older sister's boyfriend routinely spent the night there, and her parents encouraged them to share a room together. I plan to encourage my kids to hold off until marriage before consummating love relationships. And I plan to teach them why, to let them know how sacred sexuality is, how, when seen correctly, our capacity to give and receive physical love is one of the greatest gifts God has granted us.

Adult sites cheapen that gift. But they also expose that cheapening, thereby enhancing our appreciation of the gift in its purer forms. Similarly, hate sites help us to expose and root out the hatred in society, and in ourselves.

If evil is to be defined as that place where sanctity is hidden, then as more such places are exposed, the less hidden God becomes. The secret places belong to God, but the places that are revealed, they are for us, and they help bring sanctity to us. As the light shines on each new adult site, the glut of such sites increases and what was once exotic and forbidden becomes as dull as those ladies of the Amsterdam night.

In old-time neighborhoods, folks still hang their linen on the line. Occasionally there is some dirty linen for all the neighbors to see. The Net is just like those old neighborhoods; these sites are our dirty linen. The more the neighbors see it, the less threatening it becomes; because the more people who see it, the more inclined we'll all be to clean it up.

I recall the musical *Fiddler on the Roof* when I think of how the Net normalizes life in our little cybervillage of Anatevka. That old-time village had its quirky types; we have ours. They had Yenta the Matchmaker; well, we have our yentas (Matt Drudge and all those uncontrolled, unaccountable rumor mills) and our matchmakers (try out *www.love.com* and any number of other personals options). They had their Nahum the Beggar, we have access to the entire world's injustices, and from our own homes can do something about them. They had their hookers and cossacks. So do we. As we expose them, they become part of our tapestry. The Internet is doing that to racism, to lust, to greed, to gossip, to all that is evil and all that is good, too. What is hidden is dangerous; what is familiar can be controlled. There is so much evil out there, how could its proliferation actually be its undoing? I can't answer for each site. With adult sites there are levels of depravity (like kiddie porn) that make me want to scream, but the cumulative effect is that the more exposure, the better.

To summarize: The glut of "evil" sites on the Web (1) normalizes what is natural and thereby removes some of the temptation to do evil; and (2) exposes that which is most depraved within the world and within ourselves and motivates us to do something about it. If I heard about kiddie porn on *60 Minutes*, I'd get angry. If I saw it on my computer at home, not as filtered by Mike Wallace but directly from the perpetrator, I'd be far more likely to take action to stop it. There is some dirty linen that must be cleaned up—for that to happen, it must be first hung up on the line in my backyard long enough to be noticed.

Tonight I became educated as to the impact of hate groups in America, from the comfort of my own study. Tonight, neo-Nazis got past the door and entered my home. Without the Internet, I'd likely have seen something about the National Alliance on the news at some point or perhaps read some leaflets. But I've never been as sensitive to the nature of the problem as I am tonight. Why? Because I didn't just hear about the N.A., I met them. They were in my house. They tried to get into my mind. I saw the face of evil first-hand. There is nothing hidden anymore.[44]

What is revealed belongs to us. The free flow of information has, within only a few short years, contributed to the downfall of totali-tarianism all over the world. Those who wish to continue to enslave the minds of their followers know this and are trying desperately to block access to the Internet among their populations (unfortunately this list now includes some Ultra-Orthodox rabbis in Israel, who have declared the Net off-limits to their followers). But they will come around. As the world becomes increasingly united in this flow of ideas, we have less to fear of the hate groups gaining a sub-stantial following. The increased capacity of filters will help us regu-late some of what our children see (much as the emanation of *Tiferet*, keeps us from the pure oxygen of *Chochmah* and *Binah*), but for adults access should remain as unadulterated as possible.[45]

We read in Job 37 this bit of advice from God, speaking out of the whirlwind: "Have you ever in your life commanded the morning or taught the dawn its place? Have you penetrated the hidden depths of the sea or gone to plumb the deep? Have you seen the gates of the shadow of death? Tell, if you know all. What is the path where the light dwells? And darkness, where is its place, that you may take it to its boundary, that you may understand the paths of its home."

The voice from the whirlwind is mocking the human being. God, like us, has seen unspeakable evil in our generation, evil committed by evil human beings. It has always been our task to rid the world of it. No longer does it suffice for God stand idly by playing hopscotch with Leviathan while innocent children die. So God is helping us, giving us the tools to finish the job. I read this passage differently now.

"Have you seen the gates of the shadow of death?"
Yes, and above them were the words, "Arbeit Macht Frei."
"What is the path where the light dwells?"
The path of Hashmal, the electronic prophet You have arranged for us. And the path of interconnection that we are forging, that brings joy into our midst.
"And darkness, where is its place, that you may take it to its boundary and understand the paths of its home?"
The darkness is right here, with us, within You, normal and exposed, increasingly exposed as Your presence unfolds.
"Have you penetrated the hidden depths of the sea and gone to plumb the deep?"
That's what I'm doing right now, Lord, and it is late.

But I can take no more. I must come up for air again.

I am utterly exhausted and still a bit confused. But if God once claimed to have hidden His face from evil, I go to sleep comforted that the dawn is arriving, and that God's countenance is beginning to shine down on our world again.

23

Layers of God:
Reflections on the Art
of Online Questing

It is said of a certain Talmudic master
that the paths of Heaven were as
bright to him as the streets of his
native town. Hasidism inverts the
order: It is a greater thing if the
streets of a person's town are as
bright to him as the paths of Heaven.
For it is here, where we stand, that
we should try to make shine the light
of hidden divine life.

—Martin Buber, *The Way of Man*

*A*nd so, we dive.

No longer do we skim the surface like that surfing *alef,* half above and half within the watery face of the deep. No longer are we the *alef,* that elementary, binary creature that lives the life of 1 and 0 and forms the opening between what is above and what is below. As we dive into the waters of cyberspace, those 0s and 1s take on intelligible meaning, and just as with the evolving *Sefirot,* God's inner life comes more clearly into focus the deeper we go.

Kabbalists (and most Jewish exegetes, for that matter) look at any sacred text and peel away four layers of meaning, which I've made reference to in this book. First there is the simple, literal meaning of the text, what is known as *peshat.* Then comes the less obvious, "hinted at" meaning, called *remez.* Deeper yet is the interpretive meaning, called *drash.* Finally, we get to the pièce de résistance, that which every mystic is seeking, the treasure known as *sod,* which literally means "hidden," or "secret." There the searcher can find clues as to the very nature of all reality, the inner life of God. Together, these four interpretive methods are referred to by the acronym "PaRDeS," a word that in Hebrew means "orchard." All of these interpretive tools are helpful to us as we embark on journeys through the depths of cyberspace in search of the digital God.

I've presented two complementary ways of looking for God online. One is to look for God *on* the Internet, that is, to look for divine messages, sacred inspiration, interpersonal and communal connection, theological education and heavenly comfort as we delve into cyberspace. The other is to see God *as* the Internet (metaphorically, not exclusively), recognizing that the whole of cyberspace, when seen organically, can bring us closer to understanding and experiencing the sacred.

What are some of the things I've learned about the art of online questing through our journeys thus far?

There is a difference between a spiritual journey and a tour. When we think of a tour, we think of the natural requisites: a camera, Bermuda shorts, traveler's checks and, from the guide, some earthy quips about the locals. A spiritual journey requires no more than an open mind and a desire to grow, to be changed by the encounter.

This growth comes both from the immediate, stream-of-consciousness experience and from reflections made after the fact. I set for myself the ground rule that no pilgrimage can consist of more than two sessions before the computer screen. If the sites aren't visited consecutively and at least some impressions drawn immediately, the effect of experiencing it on the Web is diminished greatly. If I stay with only one or two sites per session, I might as well be doing research at the public library. It is the instantaneous, unbridled spirit of being online, as much as the content of the sites, that provides the stimulus for our journey.

That it is best to rely on spontaneous "gut" feelings, hoping to achieve a certain symmetry, balancing between what appear to be opposing forces (much as God does in the *Sefirot)*, seeking broad diversity, and intuiting how deeply I can plunge in one area without losing my way.

Finally, it might seem at times that what I'm uncovering is less about God than myself. It is true that in many ways an online pilgrimage can reveal psychological insights, providing an electronic Rorschach test of sorts. I don't deny that possibility. Once we begin to see God less as an external force than as one providing unity and connectedness within us and between us, the lines between spirituality and psychology can easily be blurred. Indeed, there is a far greater overlapping of the fields now than there ever has been. I mention this here but prefer not to dwell on it. As the art of online questing evolves, it will no doubt be useful for both mental health and spiritual practitioners.

One more Web journey will finish this cycle of three, this one undisturbed by chapter breaks. The first quest, as you recall, was an exploration of sacred geography, the second of sacred morality. For this third pilgrimage, I reach out to the Source of Life by seeking greater understanding of what it means to live in God's image.

24

The Third Journey
Living in God's Image

You shall walk after your God.

—Deut. 26:17

Whosoever saves a single life it is as
though he has saved an entire
universe.

—Mishna (Sanhedrin 4:5)

*I*f there is one precept among world religions that is truly universal, it is the so-called "Golden Rule." What appears in Lev. 19 as "Love your neighbor as yourself," is repeated in various forms in later Jewish sources, by Jesus and Matthew in the New Testament, by Confucius, in Jain literature, and elsewhere. Universally, we are enjoined to love God by loving other creatures, specifically other people. One way of coming closer to God is through the performance of acts of human kindness. We see God's face in the tears and in the gratitude of a fellow creature in pain whom we have helped. These acts of kindness also enable us to come closer to God because we are imitating the kind of behavior ascribed to God in sacred literature, much like a child models a parent's conduct. This form of God-seeking is known as "predicate theology," or, in the Latin, *Imitatio Dei,* and is expressed succinctly in this passage from the Babylonian Talmud, paraphrased below:

> *What does it mean when the Torah states, "You shall walk after the Lord your God?" (Deut. 26:17) It means to imitate the attributes of the Holy One. Just as God clothes Adam and Eve, so should you clothe the naked. Just as God visited Abraham when he was recovering from his circumcision (at age ninety-nine),*

so should you visit the sick. Just as God comforted Isaac after his father's death, so should you comfort mourners. Just as God buried Moses in the valley, so must you bury the dead.[46]

Way back in chapter 5, I spoke of how our being created in God's image enables us to discover the divine through the emulation of that which is purely and supremely human; God's inclination toward both justice and compassion echoes in our own. Such deeds on our part not only bring us to a greater appreciation of God, they actually make the divine presence more palpable in our midst. "You shall be holy," we read in Lev. 19, "for I am holy." Just as the exposure of evil increases the divine presence in the universe, as we discovered in the previous journey, so does the revelation of the good make God tangible in our midst. I expect to be uplifted by this particular quest.

In corporate life, managers often complain about the "duplication of services." That's why God created mergers. I hear about it often in the nonprofit world as well, as in, "There's already a youth group in town, so why do we need another?" Well, on the Web, there is no downsizing goodness. Acts of kindness are the loaves and fishes of cyberspace. There is a feel of an exponential explosion of goodness as the altruistic zeitgeist gusts in our faces. It blew me away.

My methodology for this journey includes an intuitive mix of Excite and AltaVista searches, my own hunches, and sites recommended in the *"PCNovice* Guide to the Web: The 2,500 Best Sites,"* [47] which proved to be very helpful.

Faces of Children

If we are indeed created in God's image, then the value of a single human life—like God's—is immeasurable. With that premise from which to venture forth, I begin our journey by seeking out—why not—the Website for *Life* magazine. I find it at *www.pathfinder.com/ Life/*. I click on a photo essay that seems a perfect springboard for this quest, an expose of the first year in the life of Ella Rosalind Baker, born in London in August 1995. Her father, a photographer, has recorded every key moment of Ella's life in a journal that to this point has reached sixty thousand words, and in a series of photos, many of which appear at this site. Individually, they look like any of the hundreds of baby photos that a coworker is just dying to show you until you say to yourself, "Enough already" and excuse yourself to make an urgent phone call. But when seen together, this collage of sixteen shots taken over the course of fifty-two weeks has a stunning, time-lapse effect. One after the other, I click on the individual photos to enlarge them to full-screen size, and this little flower of a baby unfolds before me. Here she is sleeping, here she yawns, here wide-eyed and pensive, here giggling, with hair ever-growing, here in a cradle, here in a dress.

Is it possible to bond with a total stranger? Is it possible to love this neighbor as myself? Is it possible to see in her development the unfolding face of the divine image?

Looking for more children on the Web, I land with a thud within a shocking sea of new faces. I am at *www.missingkids.org*, the National Center of Missing and Exploited Children, with its database of 1,297 lost youngsters; runaways, abductions, those mysteriously missing, and to each child there is a face. I scroll down through thirty pages of faces, addresses and dates. From Ottawa, Canada, an eight-year-old, missing since December 10, 1994. She smiles back sweetly, with a mop of blonde hair and an air of trusting innocence: She could easily pass for Ella at five.

The home page features a colorful collage of images as if drawn by kids themselves, drawing me in even more to the tragedy of purity defiled and innocence lost. A pastel rainbow brightens the background, and nearby there is a drawing of kids playing on a sketched map of the world before a pristine setting sun. The caption implores us to "safeguard children around the world." Although most of the photos depict Americans, there are a number from other countries. With the intimacy of the photos combined with the obliteration of national boundaries, the effect is to multiply the pain rather than to dilute it. Typically it is difficult for many of us to feel the pain of those far away. Here, the distant cries feel like they are coming from next door, like the sign posted on a neighboring telephone pole, or the posters on a thousand milk cartons. The effect is devastating. It burns the brain. It makes you care. But does it make us act?[48]

I click on "success stories" to read of some who have been found. There is a smiling shot of Samuel Fastow, who was ten when his father abducted him from his New Jersey home in July 1997. The following March, a tip led police to Alvin, Texas, where he was found and his father arrested. There are a half dozen others on this page, almost all cases of abduction by a noncustodial parent. Ella Baker's father chronicles the unfolding face of God within his child; some parents treat this gift of life with the ultimate disdain.

Does the Internet make us more sensitive to that gift, to life itself? Perhaps. But what it can definitely do is create an instant network of salvation. It takes time and money to print posters and distribute milk cartons. With the Net, the impact is global and immediate. As online activity becomes more common, I can imagine many lives being saved through sites such as this one. "Save one life and you save a universe"? The virtual universe has undoubtedly saved a number of real universes already. God's precious gift of life is in good hands here.

Choosing Life

As it is at our next site: *www.euthanasia.com.*

> *Euthanasia is one of the most important public policy issues being debated today. The outcome of that debate will profoundly affect family relationships, interaction between doctors and patients, and concepts of basic morality. With so much at stake, more is needed than a duel of one-liners, slogans and sound bites.*
>
> —*Euthanasia.com* Website

The book of Deuteronomy implores us to "choose life." This Website tells us why, in almost fathomless detail. All the key points are discussed both in simple summaries and with voluminous support material. This one site reads like the Britannica of this controversial subject. I leave even a brief encounter with *euthanasia.com* understanding that suicidal intent is typically transient, the result of pain that can usually be controlled through medication and that legalizing "voluntary" euthanasia would inevitably lead to abuses and involuntary deaths. The site claims to be accessed over a thousand times weekly and has an international flavor. It was initially part of a private submission to the Government of the Northern Territory of Australia at the time they were considering a "Rights of the Terminally Ill Act." It speaks to the issue as it's been debated in the Netherlands and Britain and two home addresses shown are from Minnesota and New Zealand. I count over 150 links to articles and testimony from medical and law journals, newspapers and magazines, organizations and governments around the world. It is an unbounded crusade for life.

I've always been pro-life, in the most literal sense of the term. I follow a religious tradition that, although it allows for such death-inducers as war, abortion, capital punishment and euthanasia, sees them as necessary only when all other options have been exhausted, and only when the taking of an individual life becomes the sole means possible toward the preservation of another life. Jewish law allows abortion, for example, when the life of the mother is at stake. Some authorities stretch that definition of "life" to include emotional as well as physical well-being. The Jewish view does not see a fetus as a human life until it is born, however, and would therefore not consider abortion to be murder in any event. This differs markedly from the Catholic view and demonstrably from the view of the anti-abortion movement in the United States. That is why I prefer that the government not enforce someone else's definition of when life begins on a multi-faith population. The role of a secular state in determining procedures for the other end of life is also problematical. Judaism allows only for the most passive forms of euthanasia, and only when the end is clearly in sight. As such, I am an active proponent of the hospice movement and an opponent of Kevorkian-style suicide.

The thrust of my faith, and the face of my God, is life. The urge to live propels all faith, whether it be through life now or in the hereafter. Cyberspace seems to represent a hybrid of the two. Its very boundlessness reflects our innermost desire to obliterate the boundaries between the here-and-now and the future, erasing the limitations of mortality. But its ability to enable us to focus on healing the ills of today anchors us firmly in the present. To watch Ella grow, to search for a missing child, to bring comfort to a depressed patient with terminal cancer so that he won't want to kill himself, that is the Way of Life.

This Life.

This pursuit of life as the highest value is manifested in divine action. A central Jewish prayer describes God as the one who "Somech noflim v'rofeh holim u'matir asurim" (lifts up the fallen, heals the sick and frees the bound). Just as God freed Israel from Egyptian bondage, so must we do all that we can to free abducted children; and just as God has brought light to the lives of so many who were depressed, we must lift up the fallen spirits of those with terminal illness. The euthanasia Website calls death "the final stage of growth," adding,

> It is during the time of a terminal illness that people have a unique opportunity to reflect on the way they have lived their lives, to make amends for wrongs done, to provide for the future security of loved ones and to prepare mentally and spiritually for their own death. It is often through facing the hardship that terminal illness brings, and through learning to accept the practical help of others that human character and maturity develops most fully. Death if properly managed . . . can be a time when words are spoken and strength imparted that will help sustain 'those left behind' through the years ahead. Voluntary euthanasia, by artificially shortening life, denies these possibilities.

Even death can be a time of growth, where life emerges triumphant. On a whim, I try running a search on Excite, plugging in the words, "In God's Image." It draws 2,147,749 hits. The first is a biblical commentary on Genesis; the second is a sermon by Rev. Adrian Dielman on Article 14a of the Belgic Confession, a sixteenth-century doctrinal statement of the Christian Reformed Church. According to this sermon (found at *http:trinitycrc.org/BelgicSermons/14a.html*) the Belgic Confession of Faith says that our being made in God's image means "that man is good, just and holy; able in all things to conform to the will of God." Rev. Dielman (I have no idea where he comes from, nor is it important) then brings up a fascinating point. This Belgic Confession goes on to state that fallen or sinful man is no longer in God's image, "for after the Fall man was no longer good, just or holy or able in all things to conform to the will of God." But that would imply that anyone who has not been saved, i.e., anyone who has not accepted Jesus, is not in the image of God.

He corrects this assumption by pointing out that the Bible itself states that one doesn't have to be a believer to be in God's likeness and capable of goodness, justice and holiness. When God says to Noah (Genesis 9:6), "Whoever sheds the blood of man, by man shall his blood be shed; for in the image of God has God made man," God is speaking many generations after the Fall. Nonetheless, God is saying divinity is not the exclusive property of the chosen few.

The sermon is grabbing me.

"Do you know what happens if we deny that all men are in the image of God?" the reverend continues.

> *What happens is that man is robbed of his created dignity and worth. What happens is that there is nothing special about man. What happens is that it becomes too easy to commit abortion, euthanasia and murder. When a man is no longer seen as being in the*

*image of God it is as easy to kill him as it is to quash
a bug to death or to kill a cow for a side of beef.*

As a vegetarian, I might go even further about the side of beef, but I'm delighted to see such an embracing message when I thought I might have to gird myself for theological battle. There's enough of God's image to go around.

Two Stories of Ancient Egypt

Three down on the Excite list is an exhibition of artifacts from ancient Egypt; to be precise, the Old Kingdom, Dynasty V (2500–2350 B.C.). Besides a keyword match, I have no idea why *www.memphis.edu/egypt/artifact.html* came up in this search, except that these artifacts add a new dimension to this journey's focus on God's image and the force that drives us toward life. For here are the images of death: a dead civilization that focused on death, that lived, in fact, for death, whose every waking moment was consumed with preparing for death, whose methods of embalming were supposed to defeat death and assure for its leaders immortal life.

In a sense, these leaders have achieved immortality. I am taken by a story of a particular mummy in that exhibition, a man named Iret-iruw (pronounced Ear-et Ear-oo) who lived in the Ptoelmaic period (305–30 B.C.). His name means "May the eye of the god be against him," meaning, "May God watch over and protect him from his enemies." The face depicted on the mummy's mask is young and vigorous; the coffin lid contains this gilded face, framed by a huge blue wig with the image of a rising sun painted above it, the hieroglyph for rebirth.

In 1987, Iret-iruw spent the day in the hospital while a medical team from the University of Tennessee Medical School examined him. He spent three hours going through a C.A.T. scan and other pathological examinations. I understand he was a very good patient. Later, an ear, nose and throat specialist looked inside his head and confirmed that Iret-iruw died of an ear infection that ultimately invaded his brain. "Also he is younger than expected," notes the site. He died at around thirty.

So the mummy eyed by the gods and named like an ear died by an invasion of the ear.

So the one whose face was immortalized in a state of eternal frozen youth died outlandishly young.

And on the coffin lid is the image of Maat, the goddess of truth and order; in her hands are feathers, symbolic of truth. By legend, the deceased had to have his heart weighed against a feather of truth in his last judgment. If his heart was heavy with misdeeds, a monster named Ammit ate it. If, however, his heart was "light as a feather," the deceased entered the kingdom of Osiris.

I don't know how much Iret-iruw's heart weighed in the end, but his sinuses must have been plenty corroded. *Ammit* had gotten, literally, a head start.

The ancient Hebrews spent much time in Egypt. It's possibly where their word for truth, *Emet,* began to evolve, and where they gained their appreciation for the need to pursue life, this life, at all costs. As the ones enslaved to build those gargantuan tombs, the Hebrews came to prefer far simpler rituals of death. The entire Exodus experience can be seen as a rejection of the Egyptian preoccupation with death and the promotion of an alternative, the celebration of life. Even long before enslavement, the end of the book of Genesis seems a diatribe against Egyptian burial practices. Jacob begged to Joseph (Gen. 47:30), "Bury me not, I implore you, in Egypt."

How we treat the dead has lots to do with how we approach life, and how we imitate God. Just as God comforted Isaac when he mourned for his mother Sarah, so must we comfort those who mourn. A direct response to the Egyptian view of death is provided via the encoded digits of cyberspace, by Rabbi Shlomo Wolbe, who left funerary instructions to his family on a Website.[49] Ironically, or perhaps by some grand design, Rabbi Wolbe's instructions were listed right beneath Iret-iruw's abode on the search engine at the time I checked. His instructions document all the major Jewish rituals of mourning, emphasizing the eternal life of the spirit and the need to comfort the living, rather than the need to immortalize the dead through the elaborate preservation of the remains. It could be found at *http://194.90.124.37/burial/mourning.htm* (although when I looked for this site again months after this journey, it was no longer there).

> *To my dear and beloved sons and daughters,*
> *The purpose of this letter is to console you for when I will not be with you anymore. A person does not know when his time will be up, but the day will come when my place at home will be empty, and you will be orphans.*
> *My beloved, I have seen many orphans, most of whom find themselves in darkness without hope. I therefore came to the conclusion that before one can comfort a mourner, it is essential to teach him how to deal with the situation. I hope I succeed in this endeavor, and may you understand these words so that they illuminate your lives.*
> *Our great teacher (Rav Yeruchem Levovitz of Mir) wrote: "Death should be understood as one who*

moves from one city to another. This is the real truth. Your father has not died, may his memory be blessed, for he is alive. He has merely moved. To the understanding person there is even more to say. The deceased is now even closer to you than before for now there are no separations. As an example, we see what our Sages say about Yosef Hatzadik; that he withstood temptation because of the vision of his father before his eyes.

"Yosef" is Joseph, who, according to legend, was able to withstand the advances of Potiphar's wife because his father's spiritual presence was so real to him. Jacob was not dead at the time of that incident, but ironically, I had just read the account of both Jacob's and Joseph's deaths in the synagogue the day before encountering this ethical will and the Egyptian artifact exhibit. To fully appreciate this irony, you've got to know these details about that scriptural portion:

Following Jacob's death in Egypt, he is embalmed, Egyptian style, and brought in a grand Egyptian procession back to Canaan. But unlike the custom of Egyptian noblemen to prepare his own ornate burial site during his lifetime, Jacob is buried in a simple, collective family burial cave, seeing death as a means of being "gathered to his people," rather than being separated from them.

The people of Egypt mourn Jacob for seventy days, only two fewer days than they normally mourned for a Pharaoh; but when Joseph brought his father's body back to Canaan, he mourned only seven days (which accounts for the Jewish custom of "sitting *shiva*," mourning for seven days).

The Hebrew word for coffin is *aron*, which is the same word used for "ark." When the Israelites were freed from slavery and wandering in the Wilderness, they carried with them the bones of Joseph in one *aron* and the Tablets of the Law in the other.

The portion that tells of the deaths of Joseph and Jacob is called *Vayechi*, "And he lived."

The thrust of this story is to contrast the Bible's quest for meaning in this life with the Egyptian obsession with death and the afterlife. If I were looking for a hidden *(sod)* connection between these two Websites, visited consecutively on that particular day, it would be through the contrasting visions of life and death. And the key words would be *"emet"* and Joseph. While I might have been able to predict much of what Rabbi Wolbe would have said, I never could have known in advance that he would mention Joseph, thus establishing the link to Egypt and Egyptian burial practices. And my limited background in Egyptology would not have enabled me to establish the linkage between that culture's notion of truth and the similar terminology of ancient and modern Hebrew.

Here's what glares out at me as the true message of these two interrelated sites:

Truth *(Ammit/Emet)* eats away at falsehood; in this case, literally, as demonstrated by Iret-iruw's premature death caused by the corrosive infection of his brain. And what is truth? As demonstrated by Joseph and Jacob, and mentioned as the "real truth" by Rabbi Wolbe, it is that the dead are present in our lives right here, in this world. They live on through us, and they continually inspire us. The way to keep the dead alive is not to preserve their remains and stash them in impregnable tombs with all their possessions, but rather to keep on living, to get on with life as quickly as possible. Life triumphs through the sheer force of living. And while that is a message I've heard before, the way it unfolded before me on the Web was a process itself imbued with holiness, with the presence of God.

Being Godlike: Simple Acts of Kindness

I return to the "In God's Image" list I had generated and come across a homiletical piece that puts me back onto the goodness trail, an inspirational sermonette that begins with the creation of humanity in God's image (Gen. 1:27) and leaves us off with the simple but all-too-necessary message, "Don't be crabby."

"When people look at us," asks the preacher, whose name I do not know because it doesn't appear in this page and there is no link to a home page, "do our natures seem like God's to them? How faithfully are we representing God to those around us?"

And here is the response.

"First, think about the people you encounter during your days— family, coworkers, employees, fellow students, many of whom are nonbelievers. Do your words, your attitudes, your reactions, reflect God's character? Would Jesus say what you say, do what you do?

"Also, remember that *all* people have been created in God's image, and He loves *all* people, including the unreasonable boss, the relative we dread seeing at Christmas, the irritating coworkers, the guy (or girl) who cuts us off in traffic. . . . Before we say something crabby to a salesclerk or waitress, perhaps we should think something like this: 'Hmmm, God loves this person. I should be patient and kind. Perhaps she is having a bad day.'"

And he—or maybe she—concludes with this benediction: "Dear Father, please help us to change our words, attitudes and behaviors to more faithfully represent You. In Jesus' name, amen."

The message is so simple that it really doesn't need an author. In cyberspace, attribution seems almost superfluous. If there are footnotes on a given article, and I've seen few of them, it's often too cumbersome to click or scroll down to find them. Once an idea is released in this milieu, it seems to gain flight on its own. In the real world this happens too, but anonymity appears much more natural on the Internet, where I am emailed more anonymous bad jokes in a week than I used to hear in a decade, and where brilliant ideas that I emailed to my congregants last week are sent back this week by way of Nebraska or Mongolia as someone else's—or no one else's.

A close rabbinic friend of mine has stated that the entire Covenant of Sinai, all that God communicated to Israel at the mountain, comes down to one thing: "Be good to one another—now you go and figure the rest out." The ancient sage Hillel also saw the Golden Rule as the essence of Sacred Teaching. "What is hateful to you do not do to your fellow; the rest is commentary. Now go and learn," is what he said.

So the preacher is telling us not to yell at waitresses because they are in the image of God. God, too, shows commonsense courtesy in the Bible, even resorting to a white lie at one point in relating to Abraham the fact that Sarah thought she was too old to have a child, when in fact Sarah really thought that *he* was too old (Gen. 18:12–13). We bring God into our midst with such simple acts of kindness.

The Website *www.knowledgism.com/becloser.html* repeats this message, even in its URL. Be closer! Love one another! The author, Alan C. Walter, defines living in God's image as meaning that man is a Spiritual Being with the potential for: knowledge, immortality, responsibility, integrity, leadership, honesty, love, harmony, power, survival, friendliness, wisdom, judgment, justice, goodness and truth. He displays these "divine" qualities in two columns, all capitalized, with truth by itself on the bottom. Truth becomes the thread linking this to previous sites I've explored. In its form, this listing appears like a classic kabbalistic depiction of God's emanations, the *Sefirot*. In its content it carries forth the message that to be closer to God, as Walter concludes, " . . . it is necessary to come as close as possible to those qualities that God has."

Did you know that there is actually an international grassroots movement afoot to get people to be nicer to each other? I'm not speaking here about the obvious acts of kindness, like housing the homeless, feeding the hungry and attending to the dying. I'm referring to those little, virtually unnoticeable acts, like the white lie God told to Abraham, like paying the toll for the three cars behind you, leaving a muffin and thank-you note for your garbage collector or helping a person load groceries into the car. These seemingly small gestures have a way of feeding off of themselves, until, theoretically at least, they bring us to greater levels of goodness. This movement is spreading, to the point where it is sprouting up independently, as if on some divine cue, all over the world.

I gave a major sermon on this subject recently on the Jewish New Year. I had been cued into a movement to promote simple gestures of goodness by a bumper sticker I saw on a rundown station wagon while vacationing on Cape Cod the previous summer. It stated, "Perform Random Acts of Kindness and Senseless Acts of Beauty." I then happened to have previewed an educational video on goodness in which the same bumper sticker appeared. I called the producers of the video, hoping to procure a few hundred such stickers for my congregants, only to discover that they had no idea where it originated. After the sermon was given, a congregant informed me that this Random Acts thing is very big—it's even been featured on *Oprah*.

Had I checked the Internet at the time (didn't—a victim of yesterday's thinking) I'd have found a world filled with Random Acts of Kindness. I'd have seen that the movement has a name (RAK), a foundation and even an annual week of observance (Random Acts of Kindness Week) that is celebrated by millions of people in the United States, Canada, Scotland, England and Australia. I'd have discovered that over four hundred churches participate, along with seventy-five hundred schools, and that on Long Island, forty-four thousand Girl Scouts pledged to perform random acts of kindness. And I'd have read a most moving explanation of the purpose of this movement, written by Daphne Rose Kingma, found in a book she wrote on the subject and at *www.ReadersNdex.com/randomacts/whatis.html:*

To become the perpetrator of Random Acts of Kindness, then, is to become in some sense an angel. For it means you have moved beyond the limits of your daily human condition to touch wings with the divine. No longer circumscribed by can and must, you have set your soul free to give for the sheer beautiful sake of true giving. In giving freely, purely, for no reason and every reason, you move into another person's emotional landscape—not because you must, not because you have no choice, but because in your heart, that majestically super-human organ, you have felt the spiritual necessity of acting out your love. To become the person who behaves in this way is to be twice blessed.

For, in enacting these beautiful, spontaneous, wholly gratuitous goodnesses, you transform not only the world, but yourself.

It would have been enough for me to stop here. But a search for "Random Acts of Kindness" took me to a number of sites, many of which had no relation with Kingma's. From Tennessee, an evangelical "Conspiracy of Kindness" page, an interactive Web magazine called "Spreading Kindness," based in Colorado, a "Good Neighbor Day," during which people randomly distributed roses to express goodwill, and a "Love Your Neighbor" campaign out of Miami (they were the ones who got *www.loveyourneighbor.com*, in case you wondered, at least at the time I made this journey). And then there is this otherwise-unidentified Libertarian at another site who describes how he got turned on to the Random Acts of Kindness. He was having a last walk in the Upper Peninsula of Michigan with a close female friend before departing to seek his fortune in Finland. "As we walked we came upon a small bottle," he continues. "It just looked like a salt shaker, but we picked it up anyway. Upon closer inspection, we discovered that it was a message in a bottle. Just a little missive sent from one person to another, randomly."

Isn't that just what the Web is, I wonder—so many messages from so many bottles, so many random cries from so many random people. This particular missive is duplicated on the site in a large picture file that I download. The borders of the page are sky blue, with winding pink ribbon and yellow and pink flowers. Two hearts are emblazoned on the bottom, connected by a rainbow. On one of the hearts is a leaping unicorn. In lovely, tender calligraphy, the letter reads,

Douglas,
When the world looks dark
And happiness fades to tears
Remember your friends
The hugs and love
They shall carry you
Thru the years
Hearts connected by rainbows
Your friend forever,
—Kristi Shrank

"I thought that I might like to tell people about the wonderful message that I had found," he adds. "The Web seemed the perfect place for such a story. I had hoped that somebody had created a Random Acts of Kindness homepage. I searched, but there were none being maintained at that time. My philosophy of the Web has been that if you are trying to find a page on a certain subject and you cannot find one, it is somehow your duty to create one. Well, here it is!"

Has this man ever heard of Daphne Rose Kingma, or the 1993 book that got the RAK movement going, or even the appearance on *Oprah*? Was he aware of the global nature of this movement, that not long ago, RAK movements from seven continents met in Tokyo to share ideas and ended up forming a global kindness alliance? Apparently not, but neither was I. All I knew was that a bumper sticker and an instructional video carried a great idea. All he knows here is that just as he was about to say good-bye to someone very special, he and she were given a message written by another for another, yet meant especially for them. Our words and deeds are like that. Once released to the world, the impact they have can be most profound, and never known to the one who released them. Words released in a bottle might change a single life, just as words shouted over a canyon will reverberate back to one person, at one time only. But words seared onto a Website can echo until eternity.

Where do we find God? Where people do God-like things. And what are some more of the God-like things people can do? In addition to those listed in the passage at the beginning of this chapter, visiting the sick, clothing the naked and comforting mourners. Jewish texts speak elsewhere of the sacred nature of such specific activities as providing hospitality, leaving crops at the corner of one's field for the poor, not putting a stumbling block before the blind and making peace between people. In one Talmudic passage describing many of these meritorious acts, the text then concludes (Shabbat 127b), "And the study of Torah is basic to them all."

With the Internet as our "Torah," for the final leg of our journey we run through some more of these divine qualities as manifested in human action, and this quick study grants us just a peek at the Web's vast potential to sanctify our lives.

Visiting the Sick

Did you know that some doctors still do house calls? Virtual house calls, that is. I pay a visit to *www.dr.greene.com* (no longer at that address, last I checked) and find "pediatric wisdom for the information age." "Whether you're looking for help with ear infections, rashes, bedwetting or how to parent an energetic toddler you're likely to find it here," the site boasts. He conducts a daily live chat from the site and offers loads of advice, but with a disclaimer: the page is no substitute for "medical care or your doctor's attention." I wonder if a Website can be sued for malpractice. Still, the idea that house calls are, in some form, still possible, and in light of the alternative (which is to haul a screaming child to a pediatric waiting room where you might have to wait for an hour among a dozen other contagious screamers), makes Dr. Greene's a comforting presence on my screen. There are many maladies that he can cure, even if he can't yet check out my child's ear canal. He may not be able to now, but others can. Undoubtedly, the technology of distance healing, already found in hospitals, will soon make it into the home.

Feeding the Hungry

World Hunger Year (*www.worldhungeryear.org*) has been doing the Lord's work since it was cofounded years ago by the renowned singer-storyteller Harry Chapin, who died tragically in 1981. I read the site's goals with great interest, then run a search for "hunger" on AltaVista. The result: 252,630 hits on food banks everywhere, featuring everything from abject poverty to eating disorders. Hunger, I learn, is not a purely physical state, but rather primarily a spiritual one. I'm especially moved by a brief book review by a young girl, choosing to use the Web as her therapy group, reaching out to be alone/together with us. She is responding to Amazon.com's invitation for young readers of a book about a girl who suffers from anorexia to submit responses. While she uses her actual name on the site, I refrain from releasing it into the colder noncyber world. *Book rating:* **** *four stars (incredible)*

What is this book about? Hunger Point *is about a girl whose sister dies of anorexia. Frannie, the main character (whose sister dies), tells her feelings on how she dealt with it.*

What did you like about the book? *I liked the book because I was diagnosed with anorexia. It really pulled me back on track.*

> Was there anything you didn't like about the story or the writing style? *The only thing I didn't like about the novel was that a good amount of curses were used.*
> Do you have any other comments about yourself or the book that would give us a better understanding of your review? *As I mentioned above, I was diagnosed with anorexia. This story made me realize the good and threw away the bad. It brought me back on track.*

I make a mental note to spend some afternoon diving into these hunger sites, possibly during one of Judaism's half dozen or so minor fast days, or as a lead-in to the Day of Atonement. Maybe I need to create another fast day entirely, to reflect on the sanctity of my body and my good fortune for having the food to nourish it.

Hospitality (Housing the Homeless)

On earthsystem.org's Website *(www.earthsystems.org/ways)*, Rabbi Charles Kroloff's *54 Ways You Can Help the Homeless* puts a human face on the vexing social issue of homelessness. Click on any of the fifty-four and you'll see a short anecdote that brings it all home. Take number five, "Respond with Kindness." I click on it and this is what unfolds:

Phyllis Cohen still remembers the homeless woman she encountered at New York's Penn Station. She gave the woman one dollar and asked her which was the nearest exit to Macy's.

"Her face lit up like a corpse come to life," Ms. Cohen recalls. "She gave me detailed directions and walked with me to be sure I got it right, talking animatedly all the way. It seemed as though by asking something of her, by assuming she had something to give, I had validated, or reinstated, her personhood.

"I think of her often, of her reacting as though I'd given her a great gift. Sometimes I consider going to Penn Station to seek her out, but I hope not to find her there."

Homelessness on AltaVista? 60,850 hits.

Removing Stumbling Blocks Before the Blind (Caring for Those with Disabilities)

I stumble across the Computer Network *(www.citynet.com/vipace/friends/chicago)*, "a consortium of blind and visually impaired people who want to maintain up-to-date knowledge about computer technology." Network members pool knowledge and resources to help themselves and each other function at their best in the electronic age.

Promoting Peace Among People

Www.igc.org/nonviolence/ is a nice final stop on this whirlwind expedition in goodness. The group's mission statement lays out an admirable path: "Nonviolence International (NI) assists individuals, organizations, and governments striving to utilize nonviolent methods to bring about changes reflecting the values of justice and human development on personal, social, economic and political levels."

To put their philosophy into action, the group trains individuals, organizations and governments in nonviolent action and democratization campaigns; educates the public on nonviolent methods for change; coordinates teams of international nonviolence trainers; supports nonviolent activists and their campaigns; organizes conferences on nonviolent struggles and peacekeeping; and works on the local level with gangs and local leaders to reduce street and

community violence. Mahatma Gandhi and Martin Luther King Jr.,
would be proud.

I am personally not a pacifist, though as a middle child, I've
always seen the merit of resolving conflicts peacefully whenever
possible. Nor do I subscribe to all of the group's agenda, especially its apparent anti-Israel tilt. But, as with many of the sites I've
hit, it's not easy to know what the group's bias is—opposing posi-
tions seem to balance one another.

"And the Study of Torah Is Equal to Them All"

A favorite poem of mine, by the Israeli poet Yehuda Amichai,
concludes with a passage that ties together the experiences of this
journey. He tells of once sitting on the steps by a gate at David's
Tower in Jerusalem, when a group of tourists happens by. The
guide points at him and remarks, "You see that man with the bas-
kets? Just right of his head, there's an arch from the Roman period.
Just right of his head."

"I said to myself," reflects the poet, "redemption will come only
if their guide tells them, 'You see that arch from the Roman period?
It's not important: but next to it, left and down a bit, there sits a man
who's bought fruit and vegetables for his family.'"

Our brief exploration of living in God's image has helped us see
how essentially human is the face of God, and how our digital con-
traption can help us to illumine that face. While so much of what
we do on the Internet might take us away from direct human interaction, paradoxically it also brings out that which is most human in
us. Each keystroke and click is a summons to our most God-like
essence; we become Midases of the flesh and spirit: All that we
touch gains a soul. Even the driest material can gain pathos when

experienced in the context of this type of journey. We can save people online, we can lift them up, we can hear their cry, we can see the face of goodness, the face of God. The undulations of the rolling, ever-evolving electronic text create a moving target, a living one, one that, like Amichai, can't fit neatly into the photo frame like a Roman ruin. Even a dead Pharoah becomes part of this living, human mosaic. His ear becomes part of the Face.

Iret-iruw's ear and Ella Baker's eyes; the groans of the dying and hopeless, the growling stomachs of the homeless and hungry; the heart of Kristi Shrank and the fragile psyche of the young anorexic. They and we are one, blended into a single hallowed countenance. I had expected to be uplifted by this quest. I was astonished by how much my expectations were surpassed.

There is an overwhelming amount of holiness on the Web.

25

No Degrees—One Self

Lord, open our hearts that we may
love each other as You love us.
Renew in us Your spirit, free us and
make us One.

—Mother Teresa

O ur society is so hungry for linkage. One indication of this is the "Six Degrees of Separation" concept, the idea that any two people in this world are linked through the people they know. For years, people have been trying out the "Six Degrees" concept on celebrities, with actor Kevin Bacon a favorite example. It is possible to link Bacon with anyone else in Hollywood by connecting him to a costar in a film he was in, who is connected to another in another film, and so on until the match is made with the intended linkee. One online group has a database with seventy-four thousand individuals linked to Kevin Bacon.

There is now a Six Degrees Website (*www.sixdegrees.com*), which promises a networking bonanza for all who partake. It promises contacts, but when you read the fine print it sounds more like a chain letter (you contact all your friends and we'll help you tap into the "exponential power of their contacts"). But the Six Degrees idea begs the point.

For now, there are no degrees of separation.

I can stumble across Kevin Bacon's Websites (and there are dozens devoted to him), and find out all about him, and he can stumble across my synagogue's and read what I have to say. Should he desire to, Kevin Bacon could perceive at least a glimmer of my wisdom's *hashmal* and pierce the depth of my soul. And I could see Kevin's soul dancing in the blips and beeps of my computer screen, too, and maybe form a study group with him and that pastor, Kenneth Dobson. And the more I find out about them, the more I'll realize that they are like me.

And the more I see that they are like me, the more I'll realize that they are extensions of me.

And the more I see that, the more I'll understand that all of us, those online and off, are extensions of God.

The following poem by Sri Aurobindo predates the computer era by a generation. His Website biography informs us that this Hindu spiritual master "left his body" in 1950. But his words, like Hananiah ben Teradyon's flaming letters, fly free, in the blazing universe that we all inhabit.

The One Self

All are deceived, do what the One Power dictates,
Yet each thinks his own will his nature moves;
The hater knows not 'tis himself he hates,
The lover knows not 'tis himself he loves.
In all is one being many bodies bear;
Here Krishna flutes upon the forest mood,
Here Shiva sits ash-smeared, with matted hair.
But Shiva and Krishna are the single God.
In us too Krishna seeks for love and joy,
In us too Shiva struggles with the world's grief.
One Self in all of us endures annoy,
Cries in his pain and asks his fate's relief.

My rival's downfall is my own disgrace;
I look on my enemy and see Krishna's face.

—Sri Aurobindo, *Collected Poems*

There are no degrees of separation. Our souls, distinct and unique though they are, are all intertwined in a universal Web of Life, one that encompasses all the oceans and their waves, the cities and their patchwork neighborhoods, our parents and our children, and one that obliterates boundaries and dissolves masks. It is a Web that promises freedom—and delivers.

Our three journeys have taken us to three emanations of God: We've scaled the landscape of sacred place, probed the limits of divine rectitude and explored the contours of divinity as expressed in life and human goodness. With the mileposts of geography, morality and humanity behind us, other journeys beckon, and questions abound. We've left in the dust those tired old images of the Lord as shepherd and old-man-in-the-sky, and have begun to make our acquaintance with the Digital God.

But to paraphrase Ecclesiastes, there is a time to be online and a time to be off. I glance over my right shoulder as I write this, and it is an absolutely gorgeous spring day outside. It calls to me with a serene late-April breeze, much more invigorating than the muezzin-like drone of my machine informing me that I've got new email. Even minus the shepherd, the magical call of the meadow awakens the soul from its slumber.

There is, in the end, a time to discover life by returning to what is really real, and to revel in the soft buds of springtime that God has given to us all.

 **Notes**

Below are some explanatory notes and citations of sources. I've been able track down origins of most of the significant quotes found in this book, but please keep in mind that this is not intended to be a scholarly work. Rather, this is a work of passion and spiritual searching, based on many years of reflection and inquiry. Some of the ideas trace themselves back to sermons given and notebooks completed long ago. No doubt even I have forgotten some of the sources of lessons that have influenced me greatly.

1. While I've discovered a number of guides to religious sites on the Internet, I've found astonishingly few depicting the experience of being online itself as being imbued with great religious potential. One solid entry into this field is *The Soul of Cyberspace,* by Jeff Zaleski (San Francisco: Harper San Francisco, 1997). In this book, Zaleski both shows us the key sites for various faith groups and discusses the more general questions regarding seeking spirituality online. On the whole,

however, why are books like this one the exception to the rule, and why have virtually none been written by mainstream religious leaders? Religious traditions are notoriously conservative in confronting societal change, and the religious establishment is primarily still too uncomfortable with the technology to seek God's presence there. Meanwhile, hi-tech culture has been historically skeptical about spirituality, although that is changing. At long last, the Nerd and the Word are coming closer together.

2. My teacher, Dr. Neil Gillman, has helped me to better understand the symbolic language we use when we speak of God. His book, *Sacred Fragments: Recovering Theology for the Modern Jew* (Philadelphia: Jewish Publication Society, 1990) provides excellent background on this topic, particularly chapter 4.

3. This famous Hasidic quote can be found in several sources. I located it in Simha Raz's collection, *Hasidic Wisdom: Sayings from the Jewish Sages,* translated by Dov Peretz Elkins and Jonathan Elkins (Northvale, N.J.: Jason Aronson, 1997).

4. Joseph Soloveitchik's classic commentary on Adam 1 and 2 is entitled "Lonely Man of Faith," published in *Tradition,* 7 (Summer 1965). Adam 1 seeks majesty, knowledge and control of the world, while Adam 2 enters into a "covenantal community," emphasizing interdependence and friendship. There is a little of each Adam in all of us.

5. The quote from Octavio Paz comes from "The Channel and the Signs," *Alternating Current,* (1967).

6. Archibald MacLeish's words were originally published in "The Great American Frustration," in *Saturday Review* (New York, July 9, 1968).

7. Tom Lehrer's song "Pollution" appeared in his album *That Was the Year That Was,* in 1965.

8. Marshall McLuhan's quote is found in his book, *Understanding Media* (1964), reissued in paperback in 1994 by MIT Press, with an introduction by Lewis Lapham.

9. Suzanne Stein was quoted in a front-page article in the *New York Times,* Thursday, May 21, 1998.

10. And we do. An April 2000 article by Lisa Singhania of the Associated Press says that across the country, groups are turning to pagers to provide twenty-four—hour support to those in need of prayer. The simple beep or buzz of a pager is intended to remind an ailing person that she is not alone. Sometimes people punch in a number code that stands for a specific message. When Merle Den Bleyker was recuperating from cancer surgery, his pager used the numbers 77, which corresponded to the letters *PP* on a phone dial, and stood for "peace prayer." The pager delivered the message of healing hundreds of times during his months of recovery. "It really was an instrument in God's hands,"

he said. "It was simply a message . . . that someone cared, that someone was praying for me."

11. For some interesting insights on the connections between technology and spirituality, check out an interview with Rabbi Irwin Kula, "A Technology of Spirituality," located at the Website of CLAL, the organization that Kula leads. It's at *www.clal.org.wkly_culture.html*. Kula was a featured speaker at the 2000 TED (Technology, Entertainment and Design) Conference, an annual event described as a "who's who of tech movers and shakers." In the article, Kula describes these technology leaders as "disconnected from religious institutions," yet "so many talked of yearning for purpose connection, possibility and making for a better world." He continues, "It's just that the pat answers of religious systems and their inherited myths are no more sufficient in the life of this new epic than bloodletting was after the discovery of the microbe."

12. This book presents a decidedly unconventional approach to seeking God. In preparing for this journey, it's not a bad idea for you to bone up on the theological foundations upon which all this is based. For centuries, theologians have searched longingly for proof of God's presence in the universe. In 1270, Thomas Aquinas posited five such proofs in his *Summa Theologica*. These five classic approaches, which have so influenced Western theology through the years, include the cosmological, ontological, teleological, moral and experiential arguments. Now you can read Aquinas's

proofs in, of all places, his own Website online. I found it at *www.fordham.edu/halsall/source/aquinas3.html*.

13. Richard Rubenstein, as quoted in his book, *Morality and Eros* (New York: McGraw-Hill, 1970).

14. Yitz Greenberg's philosophy is summed up most recently in conversations he had with Shalom Freedman in the book, *Living in the Image of God: Jewish Teachings to Perfect the World* (Northvale, N.J.: Jason Aronson Press, 1998). I am deeply indebted to him also for some of the concepts discussed later in this book, in chapter 24, on living in God's image.

15. Daniel Matt's fascinating study *God and the Big Bang* (Woodstock, Vt.: Jewish Lights Publishing, 1996).

16. Robert Putnam's article, "Bowling Alone: America's Declining Social Capital," was first printed in the *Journal of Democracy* (Johns Hopkins University Press, 1995). I read it, excerpted, at *http://usiahq.usis.usemb.se/journals/itdhr/0796/ijde/putnam.htm.* Putnam has expanded the article to book length and has just published it as *Bowling Alone: The Collapse and Revival of American Community* (Simon and Schuster, 2000).

17. According to the *Wall Street Journal* European Edition of Thursday, March 9, 2000, citing the Dublin-based Nua Internet Surveys, Ltd. (*www.nua.com*), as of 1995 approximately 26 million people worldwide were online at any one time. By February 2000, that number had increased to approximately ten times that.

18. In the Talmud, the ancient sages speculated on what God does all day, concluding that much of that time is spent arranging marriages. This delicate task was taken on by professional matchmakers in traditional Jewish society. They were sensitive, discreet people (unlike Yenta of *Fiddler on the Roof* fame), who would find the right man for the right woman. Now, that most difficult of sacred tasks has been taken over, quite successfully, by the latest version of computer dating, the online matching service. There are many. One Jewish service, *Jdate.com:* The Jewish Singles Network, boasts over one hundred thousand members, and I know personally of a number of success stories.

    The wedding I did was for Darlene Kaufman and Larry Hornstein, whose online courtship is chronicled in an article by Alexandra Wall, entitled "Got Pic?" in the June 1999 issue of *Moment Magazine*. At their nuptials, I commented on God's being present in their miracle of their electronic rendezvous. In the article, Wall explains the growing popularity of online dating by quoting thirty-three-year-old journalist Evan Gahr, who says, "It used to take me a month to meet a new girl, and now I can do it in fifteen minutes without leaving my apartment or even putting on a clean shirt."

19. People are browsing in droves in the religion section. A 1998 study by the Barna Research group (quoted in the *New York Times* of 6 April 2000) estimates that of the 100 million Americans online (yet another hopelessly dated figure), 25 percent used the Internet for "religious purposes" each month, mainly to communicate via

email or chat rooms about religious "ideas, beliefs or experiences."

20. The *American Psychologist* study was covered in depth in the September 1998 edition of *APA Monitor*. Other studies have followed, including most notably a study that came out of Stanford University, reported in a front-page story in the *New York Times* on 16 February 2000. The Stanford report claimed that the Internet is creating a new, intensified world of social isolation, loneliness and (horror of horrors) *reduced television viewing*. Norman Nie, a political scientist at Stamford, was quoted as saying, "The more hours people use the Internet, the less time they spend with real human beings." In the same article, Howard Rhinegold, author of *Virtual Community: Homesteading on the Electronic Frontier* (Addison-Wesley, 1993) responded to the report by saying, "This is not a zero-sum game. People's social networks do not consist only of people they see face to face. In fact, social networks have been extending because of artificial media since the printing press and the telephone."

21. For more on the "Lord of Dance," see page 85 of R. C. Zaehner, *Hinduism* (Oxford: Oxford University Press, 1962).

22. The chief's letter to President Franklin Pierce was published in *Brother Eagle, Sister Sky: A Message from Chief Seattle,* 1990. But it might have been a forgery. For a fascinating history of Chief Seattle's speech, and

speculation as to what he did and did not originally say, check out an article from the February 1996 issue of *Wild West Magazine,* which can be found at *http://www.the historynet.com/WildWest/articles/02965_text.htm.*

23. Fritjof Capra, *The Web of Life* (New York: Anchor Books, 1996). The quote is found on page 296 of the later paperback edition.

24. For more discussion of the similarities between traditional Talmudic study and current online communication, see an article by Sarah Coleman in the 6 April, 2000, edition of *Salon,* entitled "Jews for Java." "In many ways," the author states, "the Talmud looks like a blueprint for Web design." She then adds, "On a typical Talmud page, these writings (Gemara) are placed in discrete blocks in a tree-ring formation around the Mishnah—with cross-references, links to other sections and arcane symbols and abbreviations. The effect is of a virtual discussion forum between rabbis from different centuries. 'It's actually the world's first hypertext,' says former Israeli Minister of Energy Yossi Vardi."

25. That is until this year, of course. Or next.

26. The Wayne Teasdale quote is found in his article, "Dweller in the Cave of the Heart," in the Spring 1992 edition of *Parabola,* on page 53.

27. The *New York Times* of 6 April 2000 documents this trend in an article by Lori Leibovich entitled, "That

Online Religion with Shopping, Too." It tells of Judy Spiegel, who, after her father suffered a heart attack, gained great support from all over the country after starting a virtual prayer circle for him on Beliefnet *(www.beliefnet.com)*. A college professor speaks of the comfort a colleague received after starting a Website in memory of his recently deceased wife. The professor felt squeamish about it "because I wouldn't want to share my grief with the whole world. But I was wrong." It really helped him mourn her. Steve Waldman, the founder of Beliefnet, summed up this phenomenon: "The anonymity of the Web leads to intimacy." And that intimacy, he adds, fosters discussion.

28. But would Jewish law *(halacha)* allow for the possibility of having a real *minyan* online? It's an important issue because certain significant prayers can only be recited when ten adult Jews are together in the same room. Some wonder whether online prayer sessions such as are conducted by the Rasheit Institute for Jewish Spirituality *(www.Rasheit.org)* are "kosher." According to *Moment* magazine (April 2000 issue), rabbis at Israel's Ohr Samayach Institute have concluded that "a computer generated image cannot be counted into a *minyan*." What's most fascinating is that they got to that answer by dusting off a 250-year-old precedent discussing the viability of counting a Golem in a *minyan*. A Golem is a Jewish mythical Frankenstein-like figure, incredibly powerful but without a human soul. If, in theory at least, this robotic figure doesn't count because it is not really "present" and capable of human

devotion, how can an image generated electronically be truly present for the other worshippers? That's their logic (check it yourself at *www.ohr.org.il/ask*), but I'm not sure I agree with it. I fully expect that within a hundred years the prevailing sentiment will change and some rabbi somewhere will find a textual basis for allowing online *minyans*. With live online prayer services (of many faiths) now available for those in hospitals, nursing homes or sunny Antarctica, or anyone else who otherwise might not be able to be physically standing in the house of worship, the virtual *minyan* will soon be seen as not merely a legal curiosity, but as a welcome necessity.

29. Rabbi Arthur Green's commentary on this prayer is found on page 141 of the Reconstructionist movement's new and very inspiring Sabbath prayer book, *Kol Haneshamah: Shabbat Vehagim* (Wyncote, Pa.: The Reconstructionist Press, 1994). His commentary on the *Sh'ma,* which I quote a few pages hence, is found in that same prayer book on page 276.

30. Many of Rabbi Nachman's teachings, including the ones found on these pages, can be found in the book, *Jewish Spiritual Practices,* edited by Yitzchak Buxbaum (Northvale, N.J.: Jason Aronson, 1990). The section on *Hitbodedut,* the practice of "self-seclusion" with God, begins on page 610.

31. Mircea Eliade, *The Sacred and the Profane* (New York: Harcourt Brace and World, Inc., 1959).

32. Again, see Yitzchak Buxhaum, ed., *Jewish Spiritual Practices* (Northvale, N.J.: Jason Aronson, 1990).

33. Richard Rubenstein's classic discussion of post-Holocaust theology is *After Auschwitz* (Indianapolis, Ind.: Bobbs-Merrill Co., 1966).

34. Abraham Joshua Heschel's classic book, *The Prophets* (Philadelphia: Jewish Publication Society, 1962), was a major inspiration especially for later chapters dealing with the prophetic nature of Internet transmission. The particular quote found here is from his book, *Man's Quest for God: Studies in Prayer and Symbolism* (New York: Charles Scribner's Sons, 1954), and I found it also on page 416 of an excellent anthology of contemporary spiritual writing, *God in All Worlds,* edited by Lucinda Vardey (New York: Pantheon Books, 1995).

35. The AP article cited ran on December 29, 1999, date-line B'nai Brak, Israel. The name of the Hebrew magazine is a pun, meaning both "Good Computer" and "Worthy Thinking," reflecting the growing incursion of modern technology into the world of the Ultra-Orthodox.

36. Postscript: The server for the company that had generated the guest list on my synagogue's Website recently crashed. Perhaps the racists did indeed find out about this ironic twist of our enmeshed guest books.

37. Hashmal is introduced in Ezek. 1:4. Now take a look at

the very next verse: *"Also out of its midst came the likeness of four living creatures. And this was their appearance: they had the likeness of a human being."* So out of the midst of this powerful electrical phenomenon known as Hashmal appears the "likeness" of a person. Not a real person, but a *virtual* one. The Hebrew word used here is *d'moot.* That word appears thirteen times in the entire Hebrew Bible—ten of those occurrences are in Ezekiel, and six of them are in this chapter. The recurrence of this motif of virtuality is fascinating, especially when one looks at another place where *d'moot* appears, this time in the first person-plural form. In Gen. 1:26, God enlists unknown others (angels? divine emanations?) in the creation of humanity: "And God said, Let us make the human being in our image, after our likeness," in the Hebrew, *"B'tzalmaynu k'd'mootaynu."* The human being is created in God's image, in God's *"d'moot."* If we put all this together, we see that out of the midst of this Hashmal comes a slew of virtual images, one of which is in the *d'moot* of a human, who in turn, we learn from Genesis, is created in the *d'moot* of God. It's God's image that shines forth from the Hashmal. At the end of Ezekiel 1, the prophet states this more clearly: *"As the appearance of the bow that is in the cloud in the day of rain, so was the appearance of the brightness around (the fire). This was the appearance of the likeness of the glory of the Lord. And when I saw it, I fell upon my face, and I heard a voice of one speaking."* Virtual divinity was not only very real for Ezekiel, it evoked in him tremors of awe.

38. The translation of the *Book of Creation (Sefer Yetzirah)*

(Northvale, N.J.: Jason Aronson Inc., 1995) that I used was by Aryeh Kaplan, a great modern explicator of Jewish mediation and Kabbalah, who died tragically in 1983 at the age of forty-eight.

39. The Sefirot diagram shown here is reprinted with permission from *The Invisible Chariot: An Introduction to Kabbalah and Jewish Spirituality* by Deborah Kerdeman and Lawrence Kushner (A.R.E. Publishing, Inc., 1986). You can purchase this excellent textbook at the publisher's Website, *www.arepublish.com*.

40. Gershom Scholem's seminal works on the study of kabbalah include, *Kabbalah* (Jerusalem: Keter Publishing House, 1974), and *Major Trends in Jewish Mysticism* (Jerusalem: Schocken Publishing House, 1941). While there are a number of more recent authors who have made Kabbalah accessible to its growing legion of fans, I find Scholem's and Lawrence Kushner's many books on the subject to be most helpful in my teaching.

41. Stephen Mitchell's marvelous translation of *Tao te Ching* was published by Harper and Row, 1988.

42. In trying to gain a basic understanding of the Internet, most helpful to me was a PBS program, "Nerds 2.0.1: A Brief History of the Internet," by Stephen Segaller, which now also appears in book form, published by TV books.

43. Here, especially, it would be helpful for you to look at

the Website *(http://www.inner.org/HEBLETER/alef.htm)* while reading this section. It will give you a feel for the texture of the Hebrew letters and the vast expanse of kabbalah.

44. A recent example of how the Internet can flesh out and expose evil is cited in a feature story in the *Jerusalem Post* of 23 April 2000 showing how my own rabbinic online discussion forum, known as Ravnet, exposed and publicized mishandling in the distribution of a notorious anti-Semitic tract known as the *Protocols of the Elders of Zion*. A tide of angry emails rapidly put a great deal of pressure on Jewish organizations. "We received a massive number of complaints," says Laura Kam-Issacharoff of the Anti-Defamation League. "The Internet has totally changed the way people are communicating," she said, noting that where they once would get dozens of phone calls from one community, they now get hundreds of emails from around the country.

45. Regarding filters: A number of religious "portals" have been created enabling people of various faiths to navigate the Internet through the prism of their own belief system. At *Crosswalk.com,* one can find out the news, sports and weather—and even do a little shopping—under the watchful eye of the Christian Community Network. Jews can turn to *jewishnet.net* and Moslems to *islamcity.com*. And for everyone there is *Beliefnet.com,* which I have found to be an excellent source of daily news items dealing specifically with religion.

46. The passage from the Babylonian Talmud is found in

tractate Sotah 14a. Also see from the Mishna (third-century source that predates the Talmud), tractate Sanhedrin 4:5, which contains the famous aphorism: "Whosoever destroys a single soul . . . it is as though he had destroyed a complete world; and whosoever preserves a single soul . . . it is as though he had preserved a complete world." These two passages frame the Jewish view of what it means for humanity to be created in God's image. We act as divine beings to the extent that we champion kindness, innocence and life, here in this life, on earth.

47. "PCNovice Guide to the Web: The 2,500 Best Sites," in *PCNovice* Vol. 7, Issue 1, 1998.

48. Check out *http://urbanlegends.about.com/science/urbanlegends/library/blmiss3.htm?terms=Kelsey+Booke+Jones* to read about a case of a missing child that has been reverberating around the Internet for months. Many readers of this book have likely received this plea. I have, forwarded to me several times by different people:

Subject: URGENT!!!
Date: Tue, 12 Oct 1999 12:46:07 -0500 (CDT)
I am asking you all, begging you to please forward this email on to anyone and everyone. As most all of you know, I have a five-year-old daughter named Kelsey Brooke Jones. We are from Southern Minnesota. She has been missing since 4pm Oct.11, 1999. The police were notified shortly after. If anyone anywhere knows anything,

sees anything, pleeeeaaaase contact me if you have my number. The police don't recommend I put my number online, but you can contact the police, a missing person report has been filed. I am including a picture of her. All prayers are appreciated!! Thank you, Amy

When I first received this, I immediately acted, instinctively heeding the call by forwarding it to my congregation list—only to discover a few days later that Kelsey was safe and sound, having been found, unharmed, only *two hours* after she was first reported missing! While this plea was not a hoax, numerous hoaxes have been uncovered, some of which are exposed in the Urban Legends site. The potential for email to generate compassion, however, is no hoax at all. Amy's piercing cry for Kelsey might still be echoing around the Net long after the girl safely reaches adulthood.

49. You can leave your own posthumous email messages to loved ones at FinalThoughts *(www.finalthoughts.com)*. The site was created by Todd Michael Krim, a thirty-year-old lawyer from Los Angeles, who conceived of the idea during a turbulent transatlantic flight when he realized that he hadn't properly said good-bye to his loved ones. You compose your final wishes, and the site will email them to the destination of your choice after your death. As of April 2000, ten thousand people had signed up for this free service. According to Krim, "FinalThoughts is not morbid at all. In many ways the

site is life affirming. We communicate that death is a natural human experience." (*New York Times,* 13 April 2000.)

Additional sources for quotes used include: *The Great Thoughts,* compiled by George Seldes (Ballantine Books, 1985); *A Treasury of Traditional Wisdom,* edited by Whitall N. Perry (Harper and Row, 1971); *God in All Worlds: An Anthology of Contemporary Spiritual Writing,* edited by Lucinda Vardey (Pantheon Books, 1995); *The World Treasury of Modern Religious Thought,* edited by Jaroslav Pelikan (Little, Brown and Co., 1990); and *Treasury of Religious Quotations,* by Gerald Tomlinson (Prentice Hall, 1991). Translations of biblical, rabbinic and liturgical Hebrew texts are my own, with the assistance of a number of excellent translations out there, including the Jewish Publication Society's *Tanakh;* Artscroll's *Stone Edition* of the Hebrew Bible; the U.A.H.C.'s *The Torah: A Modern Commentary* by Gunther Plaut (and the new commentary on the Haftorahs as well); *The Schocken Bible,* translated by Everett Fox; *The Oxford Annotated Bible, The New Mahzor* and the old *High Holiday Prayer Book,* published by Prayer Book Press; and *The Soncino Talmud, The Soncino Midrash Rabbah* and *The Soncino Zohar* produced on CD-ROM by Davka Corporation and Soncino Press, part of Judaica Press, Inc.

Talmud, p. 89